INSTRUCTOR'S MANUAL

HARBRACE
COLLEGE
HANDBOOK

TENTH EDITION

INSTRUCTOR'S MANUAL

HARBRACE
COLLEGE
HANDBOOK

TENTH EDITION

Suzanne S. Webb
Texas Woman's University

Harcourt Brace Jovanovich, Publishers
San Diego New York Chicago Atlanta Washington, D.C.
London Sydney Toronto

ISBN: 0-15-531852-7

Printed in the United States of America

PREFACE

This manual is designed to assist instructors in using the Tenth Edition of the *Harbrace College Handbook.* It includes

- answers to all exercises in the Tenth Edition except those that call for original work

- supplemental class activities, arranged by Handbook section, intended to help stimulate student interest in various aspects of language use

- a selected bibliography of current works of interest to teachers of composition

- brief, practical discussions of each of the thirty-five sections in the Handbook

- suggested criteria for the evaluation and grading of student themes

In addition to the Instructor's Manual, the *Harbrace College Handbook* is accompanied by a number of auxiliaries:

Correction Chart An instructor's correction chart, which is an enlarged version of the front endpapers of the Handbook and the list of revision symbols from inside the back cover, is available free of charge to all adopters. Many instructors find the correction chart a convenient reference for marking papers; for that reason, it is designed to fold out and stand upright on the instructor's desk.

Harbrace College Workbooks Users of the Handbook may wish to supplement it with one of the three forms of the *Harbrace College Workbook,* Forms

10A and 10B by Sheila Y. Graham, late of the University of Tennessee, and Larry G. Mapp, Middle Tennessee State University, and Form 10C by Sheila Y. Graham and Melissa E. Barth, Appalachian State University. Forms 10A and 10C are published the same year as the Handbook, Form 10B a year later. Each form of the Workbook follows the organization and, in general, the numbering system of the Handbook. In each form, the examples and exercises follow a theme (for example, exploring the cosmos in Form 10A and writing for the world of work in Form 10C) to provide continuity and stimulate interest in the material. Each Workbook contains roughly two-thirds exercise material and one-third explanatory material; pages are perforated so that completed exercises can be easily removed and handed in to the instructor. A two-color Instructor's Edition of each Workbook is available to adopters of the respective Student Edition. (The Instructor's Edition is identical to the Student Edition, except that answers to all exercises are printed in a second color in the appropriate spaces.)

The *Harbrace College Workbook* can be used to supplement the exercises in the Handbook; it can also be used as a completely self-sufficient text. Some instructors ask all students to purchase the Handbook and only those students needing extra help to purchase the Workbook.

Form 10A (1986) and Form 10B (1987) are virtually identical in explanatory matter, differing only in the theme of the exercises. In short, Form 10A and Form 10B are interchangeable.

Form 10C differs from Forms 10A and 10B not only in its special theme—the world of work—but also in its more extensive coverage of basic grammar. Approximately one-half of the exercise material in Form 10C is devoted to basic grammar, the remainder to the other five parts of the Workbook. In addition, the explanations in Form 10C are somewhat more elementary than their equivalents in Forms 10A and 10B.

Test Package   Available on request to all adopters of either the *Harbrace College Handbook* or one of the three forms of the *Harbrace College Workbook* is a new, expanded Test Package containing a total of 500 items: two multiple-choice comprehensive tests of 100 items each; two multiple-choice essentials tests of 50 items each; six 25-item multiple-choice tests covering Sections 1–3, 4–7, 8–11, 12–17, 8–30, and 31–33; five 10-item tests focusing on specific problem areas and requiring students to rewrite faulty sentences: (1) sentence sense and verb forms; (2) agreement; (3) subordination and parallelism; (4) coherence and shifts; and (5) fragments, comma splices, and fused sentences.

Acknowledgments
Substantial portions of this manual—all of the material retained from the Instructor's Guide for the Ninth Edition of the *Harbrace College Handbook*—are

the work of Eileen B. Evans of Western Michigan University. I wish also to thank Thomas V. Broadbent and Cate Safranek of Harcourt Brace Jovanovich for valuable suggestions and attention to detail. Finally, no set of acknowledgments for this manual would be complete without thanks to Mary E. Whitten, to whom my debt for wise guidance and kind tutelage is incalculable.

                                                                                            S.S.W.

CONTENTS

SECTIONS 1–35: DISCUSSIONS, ACTIVITIES, AND ANSWERS TO EXERCISES

1

SENTENCE SENSE

Grammar instruction shows students the patterns of English and provides part of the common vocabulary students and instructors use in discussing the strategies of effective sentences and paragraphs.

Defining both *grammar* and *usage* and distinguishing between them may help students gain an awareness of the system of the English language and more readily accept various attitudes toward it. Reading the definitions in several college dictionaries (for example, "*grammar* The system of word structures and word arrangements of a given language at a given time," from *Webster's New World Dictionary* or "*usage* The actual or expressed way in which a language or its elements are used, interrelated, or pronounced in expression" from the *American Heritage Dictionary*) may help students understand the difference between grammar and usage. You might also read (or distribute copies of) the following definitions:

> "The science of language is philology, or, in more recent jargon, *linguistics*. Grammar is a branch of that science, and can be defined as the branch that deals with a language's inflections (*accidence*), with its phonetic system (*phonology*), and the arrangement of words in sentences (*syntax*)." —H. W. FOWLER, *Dictionary of Modern Usage*

> "A linguistic description of some language is called a grammar of that language. A grammar, then, is a set of statements saying how a language works. It includes, for example, a description of the principles for combining words to form grammatical sentences."
> —RONALD W. LANGACKER, *Language and Its Structure*

The third sense in which people use the word "grammar" is "linguistic etiquette." This we may call "Grammar 3." The word in this sense is often coupled with a derogatory adjective: we say that the expression "he ain't here" is "bad grammar." What we mean is that such an expression is bad linguistic manners in certain circles. From the point of view of "Grammar 1" [the set of formal patterns in which the words of a language are arranged] it is faultless; it conforms just as completely to the structural patterns of English as does "he isn't here." The trouble with it is like the trouble with Prince Hal in Shakespeare's play—it is "bad" not in itself, but in the company it keeps.   —W. NELSON FRANCIS, "Revolution in Grammar"

Grammatical Terms (pages 501–27) contains much information that will be helpful to students as they work through Section **1** of the handbook—and the rest of the handbook as well. To accustom students to using the glossary, refer them to it frequently—for conjugation of verbs, for additional definitions of many of the terms used in Section **1**, and for additional examples.

ACTIVITIES

1. Students may not be familiar with the term *expanded verb,* which refers to the fifty or more combinations of the verb with auxiliaries: *auxiliary + tense + verb.* If you wish to give students practice in forming expanded verbs, write a subject such as *I* or *Jack* on the board and then list several auxiliaries and verbs that students can combine to make expanded verbs. (It is probably best to put the tense marker after the verb rather than before it as is usual in stating the formula. Students tend to get confused if they have to make too many adjustments of this sort.)

   Jack   be + eat + -ing = is eating
   have + walk + -ed = has walked
   have + be + -en + think + -ing = has been thinking

2. The patterns for subject and object complements are explained in **4b**. You may wish to include a discussion of intransitive verbs and of subject and object complements:

   Subject + Intransitive verb (+ adverb).
   Jack   walked   (slowly).

   Subject + Linking verb + Noun [subject complement]
   Jack   became   an engineer.
   Jack   was   an engineer.

   Subject + Linking verb + Adjective [predicate adjective]
   Jack   felt   sleepy.
   Jack   was   angry.

   Subject + Verb   + Object   + Object complement
   Jack   painted   the fence   white.

3. Ask students to form two sentences, using the words below. Use the results to discuss the importance of word order in English.

   Sentence 1: camping, gear, handing, is, Kate, Marcia, the
   Sentence 2: and, beside, forlorn, fountain, Jennifer, lost, sitting, studied, terrier, the, the

   Possibilities for Sentence 1:

   > Kate is handing Marcia the camping gear.
   > Marcia is handing Kate the camping gear.
   > Is Marcia handing Kate the camping gear?
   > Is Kate handing Marcia the camping gear?

   Possibilities for Sentence 2:

   > Jennifer, lost and forlorn, studied the terrier sitting beside the fountain.
   > Sitting beside the fountain, Jennifer, lost and forlorn, studied the terrier.
   > Jennifer studied the lost and forlorn terrier sitting beside the fountain.
   > Lost and forlorn, the terrier sitting beside the fountain studied Jennifer.

4. Students who can readily identify subjects and verbs in exercise sentences may still have difficulty finding them in their own sentences. A useful activity is to have students find the subjects and verbs of the sentences they wrote in Activity 3.

5. Ask students to identify any objects in these two sentences:

   > The witness told a *lie* to the jury.
   > The witness told the jury a *lie*.

   Students who equate function and meaning may identify the italicized words as indirect objects. To clarify the difference here, point out the presence of *to* in the prepositional phrase and the position of *jury* as indirect object. Omitting *to* from the first sentence without shifting the word order produces *The witness told a lie the jury;* adding *to* to the second without shifting word order creates a prepositional phrase awkwardly placed after the verb: *The witness told to the jury a lie.*

6. Have students eliminate prepositional phrases from the following sentences and then identify subjects and verbs. Deleting prepositional phrases reduces the number of nouns and, thus, the number of possible choices for subject. For additional practice, have students use such sentences as 7 and 9 of Exercise 1 in Section **1**.

   a. Among my collection of houseplants over the past five years, strawberry begonias remain a favorite above all others.
   b. According to horticulturists, the strawberry begonia is neither a strawberry nor a begonia in spite of its name.

   c. In its natural habitat the plant produces runners which creep across the ground in search of a place to anchor miniature plants.

   d. With the exception of overwatering and overfertilizing, an indoor gardener past the age of reason can make few mistakes in the tending of these plants with hairy, variegated leaves.

   e. Once, however, I did uproot an entire plant during an attempt to remove a dead leaf near the edge of the pot; because of that unfortunate mistake, I've been more cautious about grooming plants since then.

7. A word's part of speech is determined by its use in the sentence. Have students write sentences following the patterns on page 8 to show

> *down* as adverb, adjective, preposition, verb
> *well* as noun, verb, adverb, adjective, interjection
> *outside* as noun, adjective, adverb, preposition
> *near* as adverb, adjective, verb, preposition
> *like* as verb, noun, preposition, adjective, adverb
> *that* as adjective, pronoun (demonstrative and relative), adverb, conjunction

Suggest that students keep their handbooks open to the list of prepositions (pages 13–14) and have them also look at the examples of how *up* can be used as any part of speech (page 15).

8. Have students identify each word according to function and/or part of speech:

   a. If Kris has been a Steelers' fan for years, why does she want to see the Eagles play?

   b. Selecting a most unusual name for her cat, Rachel called him Zeus, but when Zeus had kittens, Rachel chose another name—Zenobia.

   c. Really! That's a likely excuse coming from such conspicuous consumers.

   d. Planning a holiday party becomes more exhausting every year; but as soon as our guests leave, we will probably begin to plan another one.

   e. Heavens! If your cheese soufflé flops, we can always eat cauliflower or some extremely tasty muffins that were baked yesterday.

9. Some suffixes that signal nouns are *-ation, -hood, -acy, -ism, -ence, -ance, -ness, -ment, -ship, -ity, -age, -dom.* Some suffixes that signal verbs are *-ize, -ify.* After introducing some of these suffixes, ask students to supply suffixes for the following words and make any necessary changes in spelling:

foot (footage)	code (codify)
incline (inclination)	secrete (secretion)
liquid (liquidate, liquify)	rely (reliance)
bright (brightness, brighten)	public (publicize, publicity)
lunar (lunacy)	note (notation, notify)
lively (liveliness, livelihood)	kin (kinship)
opportune (opportunity, opportunism)	
plural (pluralism, plurality, pluralize)	

Note: -*er* to signal nouns (*teacher, driver, baker*) carries the meaning "one who"; -*er* to signal verbs (*glimmer, flutter*) carries the meaning "recurrent or frequent action."

Ask students to think of other suffixes that signal verbs and/or nouns, to invent nouns and verbs using these suffixes, and to provide definitions for these made-up words. For a useful treatment of suffixes, see Norman C. Stageberg's *An Introductory English Grammar*, 3rd ed. (New York: Holt, 1977). Stageberg discusses source verbs with derived nouns, source nouns with derived verbs and adjectives, and source adjectives with derived verbs and nouns.

10. Have students use the present-participle form (the -*ing* form of verbs) as a verb in a verb phrase, as an adjectival (participle), and as a noun (gerund):

> He was *playing* the villain. [verb in verb phrase]
> The man *playing* the villain is Joe. [participle in adjective phrase]
> His role is *playing* the villain. [gerund in noun phrase]
> Suggested verbs: *dive, press,* and *babbling*

11. Ask students to provide past participles (adjectives) describing their reactions when

   a. a two-hundred-dollar tax refund arrives in the mail [*relieved sigh, elated squeal*]
   b. an instructor asks a question on material that the student has not read yet [*embarrassed mumble, fabricated excuse*]
   c. a personnel director calls to offer a job interview
   d. inclement weather forces the university to close for a week
   e. the last parking space in the lot is taken by someone on a moped

12. Ask students to compose a sentence with three infinitives that name activities or goals for the year after graduation, goals or activities within five years of graduation, and reasons the goals may not be achieved.

13. Ask students to identify main and subordinate clauses in the following sentences:

   a. It is the tale of a young scientist named Frankenstein who discovers a means of animating a composite corpse. —GARY GOSHGARIAN [main clause + adjective clause]
   b. If a motion is too swift for the human eye to see it in detail, it can be captured and artificially slowed down by means of a slow-motion camera. —JAMES C. RETTIE [introductory adverb clause + main clause]
   c. The nuclear tests revealed how little we knew about the environmental network. —BARRY COMMONER [main clause + noun clause]
   d. I was in the theater district once, sitting on a stoop, enjoying the stream of life, when a brisk, well-preserved man with custom-fitted pants, a cane and good coloring halted in front of me. —EDWARD HOAGLAND [main clause + adverb clause]

e. If it were not for the capacity of ambiguity, for the sensing of strangeness, that words in all languages provide, we would have no way of recognizing the layers of counterpoint in meaning, and we might be spending all our time sitting on stone fences, staring into the sun. —LEWIS THOMAS [introductory adverb clause + adjective clause + main clause + main clause]

Although several of these sentences are quite difficult, some students will be able to identify not only main and subordinate clauses, but also the kinds of subordinate clauses (see Section **24**). Others will do well simply to identify which are main clauses and which are subordinate. Students will also benefit considerably from writing their own sentences, following these basic patterns:

a. Main clause + *who* or *which* + subordinate clause.
b. *If* + subordinate clause, main clause.
c. Main clause (subject + verb) + noun clause (direct object).
d. Main clause + adverb clause.
e. *If* + subordinate clause + subordinate clause, main clause, *and* main clause.

14. To review the various forms of sentences (simple, compound, complex, compound-complex), have students spend a class period writing a paragraph on the board. The amount of board space will determine the number of paragraphs. Hand pieces of chalk to the first group of volunteers and ask each of them to create a simple sentence. Make no comment. As they finish, have them hand the chalk to their replacements, who should continue the paragraph (usually, but not always, narrative) with a compound sentence. Repeat the process until sentences of all types are written for each paragraph. Then read each paragraph aloud, asking students to check the sentences for correct form and to revise when necessary. This approach relieves the routine of exercises and promotes camaraderie, especially when done on a Friday as a review of sentence types.

15. Have students compose sentences that contain the elements specified below:

a. adjective clause; noun clause
[*She knew that this woman who sat before her had tried many criminal cases.*]
b. adverb clause modifying verb; noun clause as direct object
[*As Margaret listened to the witness, she realized that her client had not divulged all the facts.*]
c. adverb clause modifying adverb; adjective clause
[*Margaret's calm reaction, which surprised me, was more restrained than even I had expected.*]
d. noun clause as indirect object; adverb clause modifying verb
[*Send whoever is treasurer this bill from the caterer before we are charged a late fee.*]

e. noun clause as direct object; noun clause as appositive
   [*The fact that the landlord has doubled the rent means we must look for another apartment.*]

Because sentences for this exercise are time-consuming to write and to grade, many instructors prefer to conduct this activity in class, asking students to bring their completed sentences to class for discussion and evaluation.

ANSWERS TO EXERCISES

■ Exercise 1 (p. 5)   Underlining verbs

1. vibrated
2. develop
3. gobbled up
4. may be found
5. gave
6. are
7. are
8. rented
9. invade, pollinate
10. straightened, breathed, swung

■ Exercise 2 (p. 9)   Circling subjects and underlining objects

Subjects	Objects
1. waves	bones
2. friendships	—
3. fire	some
4. Answers	—
5. simplicity	actions, force
6. vitamins	—
7. marriages	—
8. store	me, equipment
9. Gnats, flies	sheath, blossoms
10. He	glasses, prayer, hoe

■ Exercise 3 (p. 9)   Labeling subjects and objects of verbs

Subjects	Objects of verb
1. idea	nation
2. art, games	rules, conventions, spectators
3. Homer	information
4. enemy	—
5. We	tasks, tasks

■ **Exercise 4** (p. 15)   **Classifying words according to part of speech**

   pron.   *v.*   *prep.*   *adj.*   *n.*   *prep.*   *adj.*   *adj.*   *n.*
1. He   struts   with   the   gravity   of   a   frozen   penguin.

   conj.   *n.*   *conj.*   *n.*   *v.*   *v.*   *v.*   *prep.*   *n.*
2. Neither intelligence   nor   integrity   can be   imposed   by   law.

   pron.   *v.*   *adj.*   *n.*   *conj.*   *adv.*   *prep.*   *adj.*   *n.*   *pron.*   *v.*
3. They pick   a   President   and   then   for   four   years   they   pick

   +particle pron.
   on   him.

   prep.   *adj.*   *n.*   *n.*   *v.*   *adj.*   *adv.*   *adv.*   *n.*
4. Of   all   persons, adolescents   are   the   most   intensely   personal;

   pron./adj.   *n.*   *v.*   *adv.*   *adj.*   *prep.*   *n.*
   their   intensity is   often uncomfortable   to   adults.

   pron.   *v.*   *v.*   *adv.*   *conj.*   *adv.*   *adv.* *adj.*   *n.*   *pron.*
5. We   can remember   minutely   and   precisely   only   the   things   which

   adv.   *adv.*   *v.*   *prep.* *pron.*
   never   really   happened   to   us.

■ **Exercise 5** (p. 18)   **Underlining gerund and infinitive phrases**

Gerund	*Infinitive*
1. Taking criticism from others	
2.	to fight back
3. enforcing strict new anti-litter laws	
4.	merely to argue for the preservation of park land
5. even saving a stranger from drowning donating a million dollars to the poor	

■ **Exercise 6** (p. 19)   **Underlining and classifying phrases**

1. <u>like that one</u>   adjective
2. <u>blinded by the sun</u>   adjective
   _____   adverb
3. <u>Crawling through the thicket</u>   adjective
   _____   adverb
   <u>of shells left on top of the truck</u>   adjective
   _____   adjective
   _____   adverb
   _____   adjective

4. to watch closely   adjective

    ruling behind the political scene   adjective

    _____   adverb

5. one man sawing logs   adverb [absolute phrase]

               _____   adjective

    the other loading the truck   adverb [absolute phrase]

               _____   adjective

■ Exercise 7 (p. 22)   Finding and classifying subordinate clauses

1. that modern processing often robs food of its natural color—*noun clause*
2. If a pitcher who throws only a fast ball and a curve ball is in a tight situation—*adverb clause containing adjective clause*
   who throws only a fast ball and a curve ball—*adjective clause*
3. What my son wants to wear or be or try to be—*noun clause*
4. Because a trail sometimes hangs several inches or sometimes feet above the ground—*adverb clause*
   if he wades through water—*adverb clause*
5. As I talked to my neighbors—*adverb clause*
   that all of them did depend on a world that stretched far beyond their property lines—*noun clause containing adjective clause*
   that stretched far beyond their property lines—*adjective clause*

■ Exercise 8 (pp. 24–25)   Identifying main and subordinate clauses

1. Practice never really makes perfect, and a great deal of frustration invariably accompanies juggling.
2. Nature is his passion in life, and colleagues say [he is a skilled naturalist and outdoorsman].
3. The two clouds have a common envelope of atomic hydrogen gas, [which ties them firmly together].
4. Transportation comes to a halt [as the steadily falling snow, accumulating faster [than snowplows can clear it away], is blown into deep drifts along the highways].
5. Agriculture is the world's most basic industry; its success depends in large part on an adequate supply of water.
6. [Probably because their whirling sails were new and strange to Cervantes], windmills outraged the gallant Don Quixote.
7. There have been several attempts to explain this rhythm, but [when each hypothesis was experimentally explored], it had to be discarded.
8. Allegiance to a group may be confirmed or denied by the use or disuse of a particular handshake, [as Carl's experience indicates].

9. Some black stem rust of wheat has been controlled by elimination of bar-
berry, a plant [that harbored the rust].
10. We know [that innocent victims have been executed]; fortunately, others
condemned to death have been found innocent prior to execution.

■ **Exercise 9** (p. 25)   **Classifying sentences**

1. compound   6. complex
2. compound-complex   7. compound-complex
3. complex   8. complex
4. complex   9. complex
5. compound   10. compound-complex

■ **Exercise 10** (p. 25)   **Identifying clauses; classifying sentences**

1. *Main clause:* Jim angrily called himself a fool
   Subordinate clause: as he had been doing . . . swamp
   Complex
2. *Simple*
3. *Simple*
4. *Main clause:* He had enough mysteries . . . sort
   Subordinate clause: which involved . . . values
   Complex
5. *Main clause:* now he was chasing down ghosts
   Main clause: this chase . . . was absurd
   Compound
6. *Simple*
7. *Main clause:* The legends had horrified him as a child
   Subordinate clause: that surrounded the ghosts
   Main clause: they were a horror still
   Compound-complex
8. *Subordinate clause:* As he approached the dark trail
   Subordinate clause: that would lead him to . . . mansion
   Main clause: he felt almost sick
   Complex
9. *Simple*
10. *Main clause:* Only this grotesque night seemed . . . real
    Subordinate clause: whatever ghosts might be . . . shadows
    Complex

2
SENTENCE FRAGMENTS

The unintentional fragment, the comma splice, and the fused sentence are considered serious errors in formal writing because they often violate the reader's expectation that the writer will use grammatically complete sentences, punctuated as such. In addition, unintentional fragments usually hamper the reader's comprehension of ideas.

A few students make these errors because they are unable to control the structure of an idea. Such students may also have trouble limiting a topic, defining an issue, and developing ideas. More frequently, however, students write fragments because they are poor readers of their own writing and often of that of others as well. They mentally supply omitted words or repunctuate without ever actually seeing the problem. Generally the fragments these students write are parts of preceding or following sentences punctuated as if they were complete thoughts. For these students, identifying and understanding fragments in contexts (blocks of writing) seems to help more than working with isolated fragments.

ACTIVITIES

1. Have students distinguish fragments from sentences by using ads found in popular magazines, such as the following (from an issue of *Ladies' Home Journal*):

   a. Set yourself free. With Stouffer's.
   b. Save a Lettuce's Life. (General Electric)
   c. Improving on the French. (Stouffer's)
   d. California Avocados. Only 17 calories a slice.
   e. And you thought Ethan Allen just made great furniture.
   f. The Benson's 'new' Faribo wool blankets are still in use. One Great Depression, one World War and One Golden Anniversary later.
   g. Less is More. (Ivory Liquid)
   h. Why No-Wax Floors Need Help. (Brite)
   i. The first dry dog food that's like a home-made meal. (Gravy Train)
   j. Introducing Cutex Nailcare. Because great-looking nails don't just grow that way.
   k. Wonderfully flavorful vegetable combinations, in a special light sauce that lets each unique taste come through. Delicious. (Green Giant)
   l. The Fisher-Price Riding Toys. Because your kids have more energy than you know what to do with.

Discuss what reasons might justify the use of fragments in ads (discourse aim, limits of space, need to attract interest quickly, and so on) or how the use of fragments affects a reader. In the items above, have students identify the grammatical structures used as fragments (if necessary, suggest the categories: prepositional phrase, verbal phrase, dependent clause, adjective, appositive, adverb). Finally, have students collect fragments from their favorite magazine ads and label the grammatical structures of those fragments.

2. Have students number from 1 to 20 on a piece of paper. Then dictate ten short sentences mixed with ten fragments. Students should write down each word group and write S or F after each. Then have students check their answers and revise any fragments to make sentences.

3. Give each student a copy of the following collection of fragments. Caution students to read the entire passage before they begin to rewrite it. Doing so will help them to plan their strategy for including all of the ideas as smoothly as possible.

Celebrating birthdays as an occasion for a family get-together. A summer barbeque or a winter buffet at Aunt Leah's. The oldest child and only daughter in a family of eight. Because planning a meal for forty-seven relatives requires the cooperation of every family involved. Certain relatives bringing their traditional specialties. To be sure. Potato salad from Aunt Catherine and corn relish from Aunt Meg. With Uncle Frank's contribution being the favorite. Pecan pie for dessert. Although there is no birthday cake and no one ever sings "Happy Birthday." To celebrate birthdays just the same.

4. Ask students to attach each fragment below to an existing sentence or make it into an independent sentence. (Follow-up for Exercise 3.)

a.   [1]As a weather watcher, I am often amused by official forecasts. [2]Or, rather, by occasional prophecies made by weathermen who seldom bother to look out the window. [3]For example, one day late last spring when heavy rain and large hail lashed the city. [4]I promptly telephoned the weather bureau. [5]To ask about the possibility of a tornado. [6]A confident voice replied glibly, "Oh, don't worry about a tornado; we're not even in an alert area."

[7]Relieved, I turned on the radio, found a chair near a window, and watched the angry clouds. [8]To my amazement, I soon saw a swirling funnel emerge from a black cloud and strike toward the ground. [9]Just north of the city, about five miles away. [10]Of course, I immediately notified the weather bureau.

[11]A short time later. [12]An important message interrupted the rock music on the radio: "The weather bureau has issued a warning that a tornado may strike north of here." [13]I smiled as I repeated the words "may strike." [14]Knowing that the official prophets were busily rushing about their work. [15]As they tried to repair their radar and kept an eye on

falling barometers and erratic wind gauges instead of paying attention to the turbulent weather itself.

b. ¹Very late in *The Merry Wives of Windsor,* Shakespeare introduces an incident which is altogether extraneous to either of the plot lines in the play. ²And which advances the action in no way whatsoever. ³Bardolph in a very brief scene with the Host announces that "the Germans" desire three of the Host's horses. ⁴So that they may go to meet "the Duke," who is to be at court on the next day. ⁵The Host seems to know so little of these Germans that he must ask if they speak English. ⁶A highly improbable ignorance on his part, for in his next lines he states that they have been already a week at his tavern. ⁷But he lets them have the horses. ⁸Insisting, however, that they must pay for them. ⁹Two scenes later Bardolph returns to the tavern with the report that the villainous Germans have handled him roughly on the road. ¹⁰Thrown him into a puddle, and run off with the horses. ¹¹Immediately on his heels, in come first Sir Hugh and then Dr. Caius. ¹²With rumors confirming Bardolph's assurance of the evil character of the Germans. ¹³So that the Host is at last alarmed. ¹⁴He is convinced now that the Germans have indeed cozened him of a week's board bill. ¹⁵And stolen his horses in the bargain.

ANSWERS TO EXERCISES

■ **Exercise 1** (p. 29)   **Eliminating sentence fragments**

1. home, earnestly seeking
2. Constitution, a single issue dividing voters.
3. His beard was gone and his hair was cut.
4. effect, not only on
5. swat—against the law of averages

■ **Exercise 2** (pp. 30–31)   **Eliminating sentence fragments**

1. a try after I had grown tired
2. to college and that all tests
3. spring fever, which
4. blood and whenever
5. advertisements that use

■ **Exercise 3** (p. 31)   **Revising sentence fragments**

Answers may vary. The following is a possibility.

The little paperback almanac I found at the newsstand has given me some fascinating information. Not just about the weather and changes in the moon, the almanac contains intriguing statistics. A tub bath, for example, requires more water than a shower—in all probability, ten or twelve gallons more, depending on how dirty the bather is. And one of the Montezumas downed fifty jars of cocoa every day, which seems a bit exaggerated to me, to say the least. I also learned that an average beard has thirteen thousand whiskers. In the course of a lifetime, a man could shave off more than nine yards of whiskers, over twenty-seven feet if my math is correct. Another interesting fact is that a person born on Sunday, February 29, 1976, will not celebrate another birthday on Sunday until the year 2004 because February 29 falls on weekdays till then—twenty-eight birthdays later. As I laid the almanac aside, I remembered that line in *Slaughterhouse-Five:* "So it goes."

3

COMMA SPLICE AND FUSED SENTENCE

Students who frequently write comma splices or fused sentences are so busy trying to get their ideas down while simultaneously modifying or clarifying them that they lose sight of the strategy for a particular sentence. Failure to remember the structure at the beginning of the sentence may result in a fused sentence; an afterthought may result in a comma splice.

Drawing examples from students' writing and explaining why the errors might have happened will help students see how the process has gone awry and which of their composing habits they must watch in the future. Teaching punctuation alone does not correct the practice of writing a comma splice or a fused sentence. Students need to pay attention to structural details—to understand how planning sentences, selecting ideas for emphasis, ordering ideas, and revising can help them avoid these errors. Once students have this understanding, they can correct the comma splices or fused sentences more effectively. As attention to structure increases, the number of comma splices and fused sentences should decrease.

ACTIVITIES

1. Have students replace coordinating conjunctions between main clauses first with conjunctive adverbs and then with transitional phrases, making any necessary changes in punctuation. Encourage students to vary the placement of conjunctive adverbs and transitional phrases. Refer students to rule **23a**, to the list of conjunctive adverbs on page 37 of the handbook, and to the list of transitional expressions in Section **32**, page 327.

   a. Molly enjoys giving presents to her friends and relatives, so she shops all year long for clever gifts.
   b. Last month she surprised her five-year-old nephew with a roll of transparent tape, and she gave him a box of fluorescent chalk for his drawing projects.
   c. Candles are one of her favorite inexpensive gift ideas, yet a single candle costs more than five dollars.
   d. Molly solves that problem by pouring her own candles, and she has made seven vanilla-scented ones and three frosted ones recently.
   e. To receive one of Molly's candles is to be delighted, for Molly is as patient in her candle-making as she is clever in her gift-giving.

2. Ask students to correct the faulty punctuation between main clauses in the following sentences:

a. In high school Laura decided that she would become a research physicist, in fact, she even knew what area of research—cryogenics. [physicist. In fact, OR physicist; in fact,]

b. She excelled in her physics class; yet her trigonometry and algebra teachers kept telling her that her math skills would never be strong enough for her career. [class, yet]

c. She listened attentively to their warnings because she assumed that teachers were expert judges of a student's potential in all fields, the fact that she always had the highest grades in physics did not influence her as much as the opinions of two teachers. [fields; OR fields. The]

d. Laura abandoned her career in physics and chose another career equally demanding now she is excelling in her study of econometrics. [demanding. Now OR demanding;]

3. Have students punctuate the following paragraph (adapted from Sheila Tobias, "Who's Afraid of Math, and Why?").

A common myth about the nature of mathematical ability holds that one either has or does not have a mathematical mind mathematical principles may well be needed to do advanced research but why should people who can do college-level work in other subjects not be able to do college-level math as well rates of learning may vary competency under time pressure may differ certainly low self-esteem will get in the way but where is the evidence that a student needs a "mathematical mind" in order to succeed at learning math?

ANSWERS TO EXERCISES

■ **Exercise 1** (p. 35)   **Linking sentences**

Answers may vary in the choice of the coordinator.

1. a. hunting; he
   b. hunting, but he
2. a. game; she
   b. game, and she
3. a. him; she
   b. him, so she
4. a. screen; we
   b. screen, and we

■ **Exercise 2** (p. 35)   **Linking sentences**

Answers will vary in the choice of the subordinating conjunction and in the position of the subordinate clause.

1. When Dexter goes hunting, he carries
2. Because the stakes were high in the political game, she played
3. Since the belt was too small for him, she had to

4. At the drive-in, while they watched the musical comedy on one screen, we enjoyed

■ **Exercise 3** (pp. 35–36)   **Proofreading**

A check mark should follow sentences 1, 5, 7, 9, 10.
An *X* should follow sentences 2, 4.

■ **Exercise 4** (p. 36)   **Revising comma splices or fused sentences**

Since various methods of revision are called for, answers will differ. The following are samples.

1. hard. Everyone
2. microbes; those microbes
4. Because . . . failed, some
5. automobile, yet the war
7. night. By morning
9. mournfulness; it
10. labor. Some

■ **Exercise 5** (p. 38)   **Punctuating compound sentences**

Answers will vary.

■ **Exercise 6** (p. 38)   **Dividing quotations**

1. "I . . . again," wrote Kenneth Bernard. "In fact . . . again."
2. "I . . . prejudice," W. C. Fields once said. "I . . . equally."
3. "I am . . . sing," Artemus Ward commented. "So are . . . me."
4. "What . . . marsh?" Gene Marine asked ironically. "Who . . . swamp?"
5. "Unquestionably . . . loud," writes Jennifer McBride; "the decibel . . . take-off."

■ **Exercise 7** (p. 39)   **Revising comma splices and fused sentences**

Answers will vary. The following are samples.

1. says, "You're
3. Johnny. Besides
4. home. In Oklahoma
6. William, who
8. right, for that happy marriage
9. Illinois. There
10. attack; however, Nellie's arteries
11. sweetheart. Then
12. want it to. Age is

■ **Exercise 8** (pp. 39–40)   **Revising sentence fragments, comma splices, and fused sentences**

Revisions may vary. The following are samples.

1. only; then
2. people. A family . . . now, not to mention
3. relay; however
4. year. It
5. √
6. work. The reason is
7. √
8. botulism. This
9. It is an argument riddled with stupid assumptions.
10. I usually buy . . . paperbacks, although I never get . . . them.

4

ADJECTIVES AND ADVERBS

Students occasionally confuse adjectives and adverbs in written sentences. The traditional explanation has been that, relying on spoken language, these students select the form they have heard in conversation ("we drove slow") whether or not the form is correct. The use of the *-ly* form in such a sentence, however, is no longer obligatory. Several current dictionaries accept "slow" (and other such words) as adverbs.

Another common problem, however, is related to speech: the omission of the *-d* or *-ed* of a past participle used as an adjective. Often, students can correct this problem once they are made aware of it. Those students who have difficulty determining when to use the participial form can also be referred to **7a**, page 75.

ACTIVITIES

1. Ask students to determine which sentences contain past participles from which the *-d* or *-ed* has been omitted.

   a. He is a prejudice referee.
   b. He tried to prejudice the jury.
   c. New Jersey is one of the few states with legalize gambling.
   d. Will any other states legalize gambling?
   e. The coach always wanted a hand-pick team.
   f. The coach hand-picked the team.
   g. We are only interested in the finish product.
   h. We finished the game.
   i. The driver shouted a clearly pronounce command.
   j. The driver clearly pronounced the name of the street.

2. Have students consult their dictionaries for the comparative and superlative forms, if any, of

Adjectives		
articulate	friendly	little
base	frizzy	morose
far	graceful	ready

Adverbs		
contritely	loudly	soon
early	often	very
likely	quite	well

Ask students to write sentences for three of the adjectives in comparative form, and for three of the adverbs in comparative or superlative form.

3. Ask students to write sentences using each of the following: *graceful diving, diving gracefully, hurried eating, eating hurriedly, gleeful laughing, laughing gleefully.*

Because the gerund has properties of both verb and noun, students may have some trouble deciding on correct modifiers. The following sentences can serve as illustrations:

She is known for *her rapid answers.* [adjective + adjective + noun]
She is known for *her rapid answering.* [adjective + adjective + gerund]
She is known for *her answering rapidly.* [adjective + gerund + adverb]
She is known for *her answering questions rapidly.* [adjective + gerund + object + adverb]
Answering rapidly, she defended her vote. [participle + adverb]
Answering the questions rapidly, she defended her vote. [participle + object + adverb]

In the adjective + gerund construction, the adjective tells *what* or *which* about the gerund. In the gerund + adverb construction, the adverb answers *how* or *when* about the gerund.

4. Ask students to distinguish between subject and object complements in the following sentences:

a. The traffic committee's recommendation to triple the fee for on-campus parking stickers proved unpopular.
b. You can label his argument illogical only if you can identify the errors in his assumptions.
c. The waves of laughter from the audience made the comedian happy.
d. Jim and Mary always say that their toddler is hyperactive, but the pediatrician always pronounces him healthy and normal.
e. As the warm front moved through the state, the evenings turned balmy.

5. As a class activity, have students identify the adjectives and adverbs in a paragraph from a recent theme. Then have students, working in groups of three or four, revise the paragraph by adding, deleting, or substituting adjectives or adverbs. Ask someone in each group to read the revised paragraph to the class.

ANSWERS TO EXERCISES

■ **Exercise 1** (pp. 42–43)   **Converting adjectives to adverbs**

1. answered vaguely OR vaguely answered
2. traveled safely OR safely traveled
3. remarked carelessly OR carelessly remarked
4. believed sincerely OR sincerely believed
5. visited regularly OR regularly visited
6. appealed specially OR specially appealed
7. nearly possible
8. unusually angry
9. suddenly popular
10. strangely sad

■ **Exercise 2** (p. 43)   **Converting nonstandard and informal modifiers**

1. seriously
2. √
3. nationally
4. Some dictionaries (e.g., *American Heritage*) accept this usage; others label it *Informal* for *easily*.
5. regularly
6. suddenly
7. rapidly
8. exceptionally
9. √
10. specially

■ **Exercise 3** (pp. 44–45)   **Using complements**

Answers will vary.

■ **Exercise 4** (p. 45)   **Using modifiers**

Answers will vary.

■ **Exercise 5** (p. 47)   **Finding comparatives and superlatives**

1. quicker, quickest
2. more quickly, most quickly
3. thirstier, thirstiest
4. hollower, hollowest
5. more modest, most modest
6. worse, worst
7. more realistically, most realistically
8. more frightened, most frightened
9. more scared, most scared
10. more inactive, most inactive

■ **Exercise 6** (p. 47) **Using appropriate modifiers**

1. worst
2. most useful
3. livelier OR more lively
4. more mellow OR mellower
5. less
6. strongest
7. tiniest
8. thinner
9. better
10. more mature

■ **Exercise 7** (p. 49) **Eliminating double negatives**

1. They don't have any home. OR They have no home.
2. I could hardly hear OR I couldn't hear
3. We never do anything OR we do nothing
4. couldn't buy any OR could buy none
5. club didn't have any OR club scarcely had any

■ **Exercise 8** (p. 49) **Correcting adjectives and adverbs**

1. published continuously . . . sell well now.
2. taste very good
3. our wettest month
4. √
5. unbiased . . . was duller
6. The mechanic who estimates the cost of repairs was . . .
7. autobiographical
8. much happier
9. very interesting
10. device of authors who write detective novels . . . seemingly

5
CASE

For some students, determining the case of a noun or pronoun must be like aiming at an invisible target—what they don't see they can't hit. After all, *cat* is *cat* whether it's subject of the verb, object of the preposition, or subject of the infinitive. Indeed, students rarely have difficulty with case unless they are using a pronoun.

Instructors may, however, wish to use a discussion of case to stress the importance of inflection and syntax in signaling meaning. Those who do might begin by working through activity 1, which provides some concrete ways to show students how case works. The point can then be made that, as the system of inflections once present in English gradually eroded, some other way was needed to convey information about the relationship of a word to its sentence—and that way was word order. This might also be the time to point out the survival of the inflection for possessive case—the only case form which nouns now display. (See also Section **15**.)

Today, readers of English depend on word order and a few inflections to tell them about the relationships between words in a sentence. Writers also use the same orders and inflections to convey information. Thus, any error in order (such as a misplaced modifier) or in inflection (case, number) can confuse the meaning being signaled.

Throughout the history of English, pronouns have changed less than any other part of speech and thus retain their case forms more distinctively than nouns do. The case forms of pronouns, then, deserve study because they carry information about the way words function in a sentence, and that information helps to convey meaning.

ACTIVITIES

1. To introduce the concept of inflection, write three words on the chalkboard: *bluckfle, rurgit, deet.* Since the words are unfamiliar ones, students are unable to guess which two are nouns and which one is a verb. Suggest that the two nouns be so marked by adding an *x*-suffix: *rurgitx* and *deetx.* Now suggest that one be marked singular (*rurgitxo*) and one plural (*deetxi*). Since in this sentence words may be ordered in any way the writer sees fit, the reader needs some system of suffixes (though prefixes could also be used) to keep the action straight. Assign a subject suffix (*deetxis*) and an object suffix (*rurgitxoj*). To review, ask students what they know about *deetxis* (noun, plural, subject) and *rurgitxoj* (noun, singular, object). Now the elements of the sentence may be arranged in various orders, but the function of the two nouns is always signaled by the suffixes:

Bluckfle deetxis rurgitxoj.

Rurgitxoj bluckfle deetxis.

Deetxis rurgitxoj bluckfle.

Next add suffixes to *bluckfle* to show that it is a verb (*bluckflev*), third person plural (*bluckflevp*), and present tense (*bluckflevpe*). Now draw arrows to match the verb with the subject and write the three-word sentence in an order other than subject-verb-object to show that inflections allow syntactic flexibility. Ask students what would happen if the inflections were removed. Then use these two pairs of sentences to show the importance of word order:

1. The cat chased the mouse.
   The mouse chased the cat.
2. Margaret is leaving now.
   Is Margaret leaving now?

2. Have students write a paragraph or bring to class a copy of an edited paragraph from a recent theme. The paragraph should include ten pronouns, five of which are personal pronouns; the copy should be neatly handwritten or typed. Ask them to exchange papers; then have them underline and number all pronouns in the paragraph and, on a separate sheet of paper, list in columns the pronouns, the case of each, and the reason for each case. For example,

Pronoun	Case	Reason
a. us	objective	object of preposition
b. she	subjective	subject complement

Students could do this activity in small groups, but guard against groups in which one student who is sure of the answers completes the exercise while everyone else looks on.

3. Ask students to collect from newspapers—campus newspapers are a readily available source—three examples of pronouns correctly used and three incorrectly used. You may wish to narrow the selection to instances of a single pronoun, a single case, or a single function.

4. Distribute copies of the campus newspaper and discuss pronouns used in that issue. If there are errors in usage, ask students to correct them, giving the appropriate rule.

5. Ask students to select the one sentence from each pair that is appropriate in formal English.

   a. It was I barbequing chicken at midnight. √
      Kim refusing to sing at the wedding rehearsal upset David and Beth.
   b. Let's you and me fly to Dallas for the weekend. √

Could it have been them, Scott and Mike, who designed the concrete canoe?

c. Give the message to whomever answers the telephone.
Jerry wanted Elizabeth and me to weed the garden every day. √

d. Professor Still is a dynamic teacher which I admire.
The question has become who should be nominated to fill the vacancy. √

e. No one could be happier than her now that the Cubs have won three games.
That cashier is the one whom she thinks the customers voted most helpful. √

6. Have students write sentences to illustrate the following:

a. *we* as subject complement
b. *whoever* as subject of a clause
c. *theirs* as direct object
d. *us* as object of an infinitive
e. *her* as part of a compound appositive

7. Ask students to convert possessive nouns to possessive pronouns and possessive pronouns to possessive nouns.

a. Mark's   d. the Department of Labor's
b. theirs   e. ours
c. women's

ANSWERS TO EXERCISES

■ **Exercise 1** (pp. 53–54)   **Choosing correct pronouns**

1. me   6. him
2. He, I   7. him, her
3. she   8. I, her
4. they   9. he
5. her   10. him

■ **Exercise 2** (p. 55)   **Combining sentences with *who* or *whom***

1. Hercule Poirot is a famous detective whom Agatha Christie finally kills off in *Curtain.*
2. Some parents who think they are protecting their offspring make an introvert out of an only child.
3. Does anyone remember the name of the Frenchman who built a helicopter in 1784?
4. One of the officials with whom the players had quarreled earlier called for a severe penalty.

■ **Exercise 4** (p. 57)   **Changing *who* to *whom***

1. Whom
2. √
3. whom
4. √
5. whom
6. whom
7. √
8. whom
9. [deceived] whom
10. whomever

■ **Exercise 5** (pp. 58–59)   **Revising case forms**

1. me
2. √
3. whom, my
4. √
5. we, they
6. √
7. whom
8. √
9. √
10. me

6
AGREEMENT

The study of agreement might begin with a discussion of number and of the formation of plurals (Section **18**). The quickest way to show students the forms of the verb is to refer to **conjugation** (pages 508–9). Although dictionaries, grammarians, and teachers refer to "plural verbs" for the sake of convenience, strictly speaking, verbs are not *plural* in the same way that nouns or pronouns are. For example, *two books* indicates two items, whereas *they swim* refers to the number of people doing the swimming rather than to two separate acts of swimming. In other words, the actual concept of plural rests in the subject in such a sentence. To convey the idea of plural action, English uses adverbs (I swam again and again), a prefix (*redo, re*think), or repetition (I swam and swam). [See also Otto Jesperson, *Philosophy of Grammar,* (New York: Norton, 1965) 207–11.] Similarly, because the verb in English retains few inflections—notably the one that indicates a third person singular subject—agreement poses problems chiefly in the present tense when a third person singular subject is indicated. The declension in Section **5** can be helpful in familiarizing students with the meaning of *person.*

When a sentence begins with the expletive *there,* students sometimes have difficulty determining the subject. Although *there* may, on rare occasions, serve as the subject of a clause or a sentence (as it does in the subordinate clause of this sentence and in such sentences as "There is where I live"), students are almost always safe to exclude it from consideration.

When the subject and verb are separated by an intervening element (usually a clause or prepositional phrase), students frequently identify the noun closest to the verb as the subject and make the verb singular or plural to agree with that noun: *One of the watches were broken.* OR *George is the only one of those waiters who keep the water glasses full.* Students who make this kind of error may have (1) mistakenly applied the rule that in a sentence with a compound subject the verb agrees with the closer one, (2) forgotten the subject by the time they write the verb, or (3) simply not correctly identified the subject. The first problem can be handled easily by clarifying the use of the whichever-is-closer rule. The other problems can often be resolved by having students identify and eliminate prepositional phrases as they proofread for subject-verb agreement.

Students may resist using indefinite pronouns in their writing for a number of reasons. Those who associate the use of certain pronouns with very formal writing (*few were turned away; each married a childhood sweetheart; either is acceptable*) may avoid using them by finding an alternate construction (*not very many fans, the graduates, both of the menus*) or may use them only as modifiers (*few fans, each graduate, either menu*). Second, students are often unsure about which pronouns are regularly singular and what rules govern compound subjects. Finally, students may not know how to resolve the conflict between the injunction to make pronoun and antecedent agree and the increasing avoidance of the generic *he, his,* or *him* as sexist. The language does tend to leave the female half of the population out, and students can be encouraged to be considerate and to avoid usages that are inherently sexist. Pointing out ways to rephrase sentences (see **6b**) can be helpful. If you wish to encourage a discussion of sexist language, some examples of sexist usage may prove helpful: ***mankind, brotherly** love, the child is **father** of the man.* In any event, you can use the development of alternatives to the generic pronoun (*his/her, his and her,* and the increasing acceptance of *their* despite the violation of a grammatical principle) to show how language changes.

ACTIVITIES

1. Ask students to identify the function of *there* in each of the following sentences as adverb (A) or expletive (E) and to revise expletive-*there* sentences by making singular subjects plural, plural subjects singular, and changing the verb accordingly.

   a. Near the fence there are five violets and twenty-four dandelions growing. [E]
   b. Hang the picture there to cover the smudge. [A]
   c. There stand Jennifer and Linda. [A]
   d. There happens to be a perfectly logical explanation for this chaos. [E]
   e. There seems to have been a mistake; I ordered iced tea, not ice cream. [E]

2. Ask students to make a list of collective nouns that describe groups of people and use some of those nouns in sentences. Explain that once the number is established, students should use that number consistently in the composition. Have them consult a dictionary to check current usage.

3. Ask students to collect examples of the various alternatives for handling pronoun references to such antecedents as *someone* or *a student*. Ask students which of the alternatives they prefer—which they think will survive and why. Students might find a newspaper column or a magazine article on the subject, and you might share the suggestions and alternatives in McGraw-Hill's "Guidelines for Equal Treatment of the Sexes."

4. Have students write a paragraph comparing or contrasting two relatives, two siblings, or two friends. The paragraph should include the following elements:

   a. one expression beginning with *not to mention* or *together with*
   b. compound singular subjects both of which are preceded by *every* or *each* and joined by *and*
   c. one sentence containing expletive *there*

    d. *one* used as subject
    e. two antecedents joined by *nor*

The elements need not follow this order, but each should be labeled appropriately.

5. Ask students to explain how context has determined the verb form in each of these sentences:

    a. All was forgiven when he replaced the broken window.
    b. Three of my neighbors jog daily, and all take different routes.
    c. Most were mailed out before the printing error was discovered.
    d. The argument is illogical, but none question its emotional appeal.
    e. None of the ice cream has melted.
    f. No apology was offered, and none was necessary.
    g. Half want to schedule the exam for next Tuesday.
    h. Do you think half is too few?
    i. Do any of the guides answer questions during the tour?
    j. Any who are enterprising will succeed.

6. Ask students to select the correct verb form and to explain their choice.

    a. Almost everybody I know (believes, believe) that football is the national sport.
    b. Marty is the only one of them who (is, are) enough of a fan to know that the national sport is really baseball.
    c. He is one of the many college professors who truly (enjoys, enjoy) the game.
    d. In the summer you can be sure that either Marty or one of his colleagues (attend, attends) every home game.
    e. Sitting on the desk in Marty's office (is, are) an autographed baseball as well as an ashtray and a dictionary.

ANSWERS TO EXERCISES

■ **Exercise 2** (p. 66)   **Choosing correct verb forms**

1. feels	6. come
2. differ	7. was
3. was	8. is
4. adorn	9. store, jeopardize
5. asks	10. is

■ **Exercise 3** (p. 69)   **Choosing correct pronoun or verb forms**

1. have, their
2. needs, she

3. they
4. was; it OR were; they
5. controls, it, itself OR control, they, themselves

■ Exercise 4 (p. 70)   Securing agreement

1. These computers do . . . them . . . them
2. a frustrated student . . . was . . . his or her (OR his/her OR the)
3. casserole or vegetables are ruined . . . "These ovens read
4. the words that come out of one's mouth are . . . the words that one intends . . . the words that one really thinks.
5. One of my instructors . . . was
6. kinds of labels are
7. are the mirrors . . . a person doesn't
8. people have . . . they actually look, not how they want
9. are other thoughts
10. does one ever see oneself (OR himself OR himself or herself; SOMETIMES themselves) as one (OR he OR he or she; SOMETIMES they) really is (SOMETIMES are) [See **21c**. Students may legitimately find the repetition of *one* wordy. They should also see from this exercise how awkward some of the solutions to the problem can become.]

7
VERB FORMS

Understanding the system of English verbs requires students to grasp an extensive network of relationships of tense to time, not only in a single verb but also in sequences of verbs. For that reason, it is important for them to realize that such concepts as tense, person, and number (as well as voice and mood) are units of a systematic description and that although these units are studied separately, they cannot be used in isolation.

ACTIVITIES

1. Have students write one or two narrative paragraphs (nine or ten sentences) in which they do not use any form of *to be* or *to have,* avoiding these forms even as auxiliaries. This exercise will reveal several important points to students. First, they will become aware of how frequently they use a form of *to be* (and perhaps will begin to use more varied language—see also **29d**); second, they will discover how difficult it is to establish proper tense sequences without these forms; finally, they will become much more aware of the function of tense in the language and of relationships between tenses.

2. Ask students to be prepared to discuss in class any problems that may arise when they try to convert all present tense verbs in an essay they have written to present progressive and all past tense verbs to past perfect.

3. Ask students to write a brief paragraph using *lie/lay* and *sit/set* correctly. Copies of the following paragraph might be distributed as a warm-up exercise and as a model for students to follow.

    Several things that belong upstairs were __(lie/lay)__ on the counter. I suppose that Sarah had __(sit/set)__ them there so that she could put them away later. I didn't do anything about them, however; I just let them __(sit/set)__ there until she came back. I did think to ask her why she had __(lie/lay)__ the candlestick over on its side, but decided to wait until we were __(sit/set)__ in the other room. We __(sit/set)__ there often in the afternoon, partly because the western exposure allows us to watch the sun __(sit/set)__ and partly because there is a comfortable couch either of us can use if one of us wants to __(lie/lay)__ down to rest for a while. We can even cover up with the afghan that __(lie/lay)__ on the couch if we want to.

4. Ask students to complete these two sentences with the proper verb forms:

a. Phil *past tense* the porcelain vase, but if Carolyn has *past participle* one, too, she won't admit it. [*bring, choose, draw, lose, steal, take*]

b. They have *past participle* sweet corn. [*buy, can, eat, freeze, grow, raise*]

5. Ask students to review the difference between direct objects and subject complements. Then have students apply the following set of questions to the fifteen sentences below to determine whether a verb is transitive/intransitive, active/passive, linking/complete.

a. Is the verb transitive or intransitive?
b. If the verb is transitive, what is the direct object?
c. If the verb is transitive, does the subject perform the action of the verb?
d. If the verb is intransitive, is there a complement?
e. If there is a complement, what kind is it?

The order of these questions is designed to show that the first task—even if the ultimate one is to discover whether the verb is active or passive—is to decide whether the verb is transitive or intransitive since the answer *transitive* leads to questions b and c while the answer *intransitive* leads to questions d and e. Thus, the choices are limited so that an answer such as *transitive complete* is impossible.

The following diagram clarifies the hierarchy of choices for students who insist on asking whether the verb is active or passive before they know whether it is transitive:

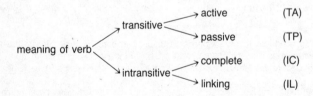

1. More hot sauce should be added to those tacos. [TP]
2. How could I have anticipated Ralph's sentence about the dead jackalope? [TA]
3. The class had been dull until yesterday. [IL]
4. I began to suspect a sense of humor upon hearing Brad identify *sea-nymph* as an exclamation. [TA]
5. Mike's days of being an outcast will cease with the end of the semester. [IC]
6. Camille went to the mountains to be alone. [IC]
7. Watching from my bedroom window, I saw her climb the tree to rescue the kitten. [TA]
8. This horse hasn't been ridden for two weeks. [TP]
9. Crystal bought a geode to add to her mineral collection. [TA]

> 10. Nick and Seth were applauded for their original lyrics. [TP]
> 11. After the moderator's long introduction, Joan began her speech on the virtues of brevity. [TA]
> 12. The chili con carne smelled delicious, but it was too spicy for me. [IL, IL]
> 13. She leaned wearily against her shopping cart. [IC]
> 14. Laughing uproariously at the misprint, they continued through the story. [IC]
> 15. Has the bill from the dentist been paid yet? [TP]

6. Some instructors may wish to give additional time to the concept of *voice.* If so, begin with a discussion of the features of a sentence containing a passive-voice verb:

  a. a verb consisting of a form of *to be* and the past participle of the main verb (*were written, have been mailed*)
  b. a subject which would be the object of an active voice verb (*The newspaper was torn. Someone tore the newspaper.*)
  c. a prepositional phrase beginning with *by* and having as its object the person or thing performing the action of the verb (this prepositional phrase is sometimes optional.)

Then write the following sentences on the board and ask students to identify the features of the passive found in each.

  a. Our meeting was canceled by the chairman.
  b. Our meeting has been canceled by the chairman.
  c. Our meeting was canceled.
  d. Our meeting has been canceled.

When working through this activity, instructors may want to point out the five main uses of a passive-voice verb [see also Otto Jesperson, *Essentials of English Grammar* (New York: Holt, 1933) 120–21]:

  (1) when the subject which would be used with an active-voice verb (what Jesperson calls "the active subject") is unknown or difficult to state,
  (2) when the active subject is clear from the context,
  (3) when tact dictates that the active subject not be directly stated,
  (4) when the passive subject is more important than the active subject, and
  (5) when the passive construction aids in combining one sentence with another.

Note: A sentence containing an indirect object as well as a direct object can also be made passive.

> The judge awarded us custody.
> We were awarded custody by the judge.
> Custody was awarded us by the judge.

From students' compositions, select ten passive-voice sentences for a handout or transparency. Ask students to rewrite them, using the active voice.

ANSWERS TO EXERCISES

■ Exercise 1 (p. 77)   Using verb forms in a pattern

1. Yes, he gave it away.
2. You have already run a mile.
3. Yes, the man drowned.
4. They have already begun that.
5. Yes, the wind blew.
6. She has already chosen it.
7. Yes, it really happened.
8. The river has already risen.
9. Yes, you did that.
10. They have already stolen it.
11. Yes, you spun your wheels.
12. They have already frozen it.
13. Yes, he clung to that belief.
14. They have already gone to the police.
15. Yes, she knew them.
16. The fire alarm has already rung.
17. Yes, the sack burst.
18. He has already eaten it.
19. Yes, you grew these.
20. Bert has already spoken out.

■ Exercise 2 (p. 78)   Substituting correct forms of *sit* and *lie*

1. Jack doesn't ever want to sit down.
   Jack doesn't ever want to lie down.
2. The dog sat near the luggage.
   The dog lay near the luggage.
3. The toy soldier has been sitting in the yard.
   The toy soldier has been lying in the yard.
4. He often sits on a park bench.
   He often lies on a park bench.
5. Has it sat there all along?
   Has it lain there all along?

■ Exercise 3 (p. 79)   Choosing correct verb forms

1. laid
2. sit
3. lie
4. sitting
5. setting

■ **Exercise 5** (p. 82)   **Choosing correct verb forms**

1. ended	6. Having bought
2. was made	7. adjourned
3. to celebrate	8. to brand
4. to go	9. to see
5. Having finished	10. has dropped

■ **Exercise 8** (p. 86)   **Correcting verb errors**

1. √	6. √
2. gives	7. rambles
3. √	8. owes
4. called	9. √
5. to propose	10. Sit

8

MANUSCRIPT FORM

Section **8** offers some general guidelines on matters of paging and format, although most instructors and some departments have their own systems. Whatever the case, class time devoted to explaining the requirements of manuscript form is well spent. As early in the semester as possible, describe precisely what is acceptable and provide examples of acceptable and unacceptable format. Thereafter, insist on the proper format. Otherwise, students are likely to turn in essays written on narrow-lined notebook paper or paper torn from spiral or steno notebooks, or even typed single-spaced on onionskin.

In evaluating what they have written, students should revise as well as proofread their prose. Revision refers to such changes in content as the addition of examples, the clarification of ideas, the development of unity and coherence in paragraphs; proofreading refers to changes in punctuation, spelling, and mechanics (see Reviser's Checklist, **33h**, pages 386–88). Both are equally essential in the preparation of a final draft. To emphasize the importance of revision, share with students the results of Nancy Sommers' study of the differences between the revision strategies of students and experienced writers in *College Composition and Communication* Dec. 1980: 378–88.

ACTIVITIES

1. Bring to class examples of legible and illegible handwriting (themes saved from previous semesters are a ready source) and ask students for their reactions. Ask why reactions to a single example vary (the handwriting may be similar to the student's own style; the handwriting may resemble that of a person the student dislikes, and so on) and how writers could guard against negative reactions. Such comments may lead to a discussion of handwriting as an expression of a student's personality and whether students must sacrifice their handwriting style for the sake of keeping an audience.

2. Have students work in groups of three to evaluate the essays of peers. Have two of the students read the third student's essay using the Reviser's Checklist. Ask them to write in the margins any suggested corrections or revisions. Allow time for the evaluators to discuss their written comments and for the author to respond.

3. Ask students to correct proofreading errors by writing the proper form above each error; have them use a colored pencil or ink of a different color from that already used in order to facilitate checking corrections.

4. For the first few essays, ask students to chart their corrections as well as the rule for each correction. Having students include the correction symbols provides an opportunity for them to learn the marking system. **Note:** Spelling errors may be included on this chart or put on the student's list of words to study.

SAMPLE CHART

Symbol	Error (in context)	Correction	Rule
cap	studying Art	art	**9f**—Avoid unnecessary capitals.
ca	Jim going offended	Jim's	**5d**—Use the possessive case before a gerund.

ANSWERS TO EXERCISE

■ **Exercise 1** (pp. 92–93)   **Dividing words**

Words that should not be divided:

4. NATO	8. against	14. C.P.A.	17. matches
5. gripped	13. recline	16. WFAA-FM	20. patron

Words that may be divided, with boldface hyphens marking appropriate divisions:

1. cross-ref•er•ence	7. guess-ing	12. e•ven-tu•al
2. e•co-nom•ic	9. pres-ent	15. mag•i-cal
3. fif-teenth	10. pre-sent	18. dis-solve
6. grip-ping	11. sea-coast	19. cob-webs

9

CAPITALS

Certain conventions vary from language to language, country to country: German, for example, capitalizes all nouns and words used as nouns; English capitalizes only proper nouns. Students generally overuse capital letters because they don't know the conventions. Occasionally, however, students will feel a need to give special prominence to a word, particularly if they are trying to emphasize its importance: *Elected to Phi Beta Kappa in his junior year, Russ is a true Student.* Although capital letters do call attention to the words they head, they tend to distract the reader and so should not be used for emphasis: *Elected to Phi Beta Kappa in his junior year, Russ is the quintessential student.*

Note: *The Chicago Manual of Style,* 13th ed. (Chicago: U of Chicago P, 1982), includes a detailed discussion of capitalization and abbreviations.

ACTIVITIES

1. Ask students to supply the principles of capitalization that govern the following:

   a. Jell-O; whipped cream
   b. Roman Catholic Church; catholic tastes
   c. the Great Plains; eastern South Dakota
   d. Freshman Composition; sophomores and juniors
   e. Levis; jeans
   f. Lake Mead; the Allegheny and Monongahela rivers
   g. Senator Nancy Kassebaum; George Bush, vice president of the United States
   h. Dead Sea Scrolls; worship service
   i. Korean War; the infantry
   j. Canis Major; aurora borealis

2. Give students a list of titles (uncapitalized) from a set of recent themes and ask them to follow **9c** as they provide proper capitalization.

3. Ask students to write down the titles of three books and three articles they have read recently (works not related to academic requirements), and three books they would like to read as soon as they have time.

4. Bring a telephone directory to class to illustrate conventions regarding names in the yellow pages.

ANSWERS TO EXERCISE

■ **Exercise 2** (p. 104)   **Supplying capitals**

1. English; I; Thanksgiving; U.S. Constitution
2. West; Carlsbad Caverns; Yellowstone National Park; Painted Desert; Rockies; Pacific Ocean
3. God's; Bible; We; Democrats; Senator Attebury
4. Robert Sherrill's; *The Saturday Night Special* [*and*] *Other Guns* [*with*] *Which Americans Won* [*the*] *West, Protected Bootleg Franchises, Slew Wildlife, Robbed Countless Banks, Shot Husbands Purposely* [*and by*] *Mistake,* [*and*] *Killed Presidents—Together* [*with the*] *Debate* [*over*] *Continuing Same*

10
ITALICS

Students who rely on italics to emphasize special meaning have yet to learn that an effective sentence emphasizes certain ideas by its diction and word arrangement and that every part contributes to both meaning and arrangement or structure. Just as the architect selects the type of exterior finish appropriate to the style of the house, so the students must choose elements of mechanics and punctuation appropriate to the meaning and the arrangement of the words.

If, however, you suggest that students try ways other than italics to emphasize ideas but do not specify those ways, students usually opt for quotation marks or (infrequently) capitalization. As a rule, these choices are equally ineffective because the problem lies with the choice of words, not with the choice of marks for emphasis (see also **16d**). Instead, students should work to master substitution (for single words) and arrangement (for relative importance of ideas). Thus, the sentence *His laugh was funny* might become *His laugh was a burst of throaty gasps* or *With a burst of throaty gasps he laughed.*

The use of italics to identify a word used as a word sometimes confuses students because they tend to see words as individual items listed in dictionaries or vocabulary exercises or as units in a sentence; they can therefore have difficulty imagining a sentence in which a word is used as such. Examples using proper names clarify the rule: *Katherine and Catharine are variations of Catherine* (compare with: *Catherine addressed the envelope*). A useful rule of thumb is that if a word can be preceded by *the word,* it should be italicized (*The word philology means "love of words"; the discipline of philology is the study of language development*).

ACTIVITIES

1. To help illustrate that different titles receive different treatment, with some set in italics and others set off by quotation marks, ask students to list the titles of their favorites: three books, three magazines, three films, three television programs, three songs. Ask students to list the titles of two textbooks they are using in other courses and the titles of two chapters from each; the titles of two journals in their major field (such as *English Journal*) and the titles of two articles from recent issues of each. Ask them to list the title of the last play or film they attended on campus and the title they would give their autobiography.

2. Have students identify which item in each of the pairs is correct:

   a. *60 Minutes* √   "Consumer Reports"
   b. *Chicago Tribune* √   Oh, Susanna

c. *U.S.S. Jackson*   *Hamlet* √
d. the *Bible*   "The Lottery" √
e. *Gone With The Wind* √   "Casablanca"

ANSWERS TO EXERCISE

■ **Exercise** (p. 108)   **Underlining words that should be italicized**

1. *U.S. News & World Report*
2. *Queen Mary; The Divine Comedy*
3. *d; t; partner; pretty*
4. *The Magic Flute; très magnifique*
5. *Battle of the Centaurs; Madonna of the Steps*

11

ABBREVIATIONS, ACRONYMS, AND NUMBERS

The emphasis in **11a–11e** is on spelling out words, for formal prose does not yet admit all of the convenient abbreviations students would like to use to reduce the time spent writing. Certain inappropriate abbreviations appear more frequently than others—the titles *Prof.* and *Sen.,* names of states, days, and months. Yet the writer's convenience is less important than the reader's needs. Abbreviation-laden writing channels the reader's attention away from the message and toward the symbols to be decoded, thus interfering with the process of communication.

The common Latin expressions (*e.g., i.e., et al., etc.*) deserve comment not so much because students use them in their writing as because they encounter them in their reading. Often unfamiliar with both the abbreviation and its Latin phrase, students ignore valuable information because they don't know how to interpret its relationship to the sentence they are reading. Further, they misspell such abbreviations as *etc.* (as *ect.* or *and etc.*) or *vs.* (as *vrs.*) because they have had little experience with them. *The Chicago Manual of Style,* 13th ed. (Chicago: U of Chicago P, 1982) 384–88, offers an extensive list of scholarly abbreviations for instructors who wish to familiarize their students with these Latin expressions.

The question of when to spell out numbers is one that students always ask. Although **11f** specifies that numbers of one or two words be written out, students often think that the numbers one through ten (or sometimes one through twenty) are spelled out while figures are used for all other numbers. Perhaps they cannot distinguish numbers in series and statistics from numbers in other usage (see "Special Usage Regarding Numbers," page 114, number 7).

The use of *from* and *to* with dates also requires comment. Students who have developed their own abbreviations for note-taking (*in 1981–82, from 1981–82,* or *fm 81–82*) may be unaware of the distinction between *from 1981 to 1983* and *in 1981–82—from* and *to* are used together, or the hyphen is used without *from;* but *from* and the hyphen are not used together.

ACTIVITIES

1. Discuss the need for clarity when using acronyms, referring to the grammatical glossary and to Section **27** on establishing a point of reference. Ask students to write a sentence using an acronym that readers are likely to be unfamiliar with.

2. Have students write sentences telling

   a. the month, date, year, city, and state of their birth
   b. their school address; their home address
   c. the number of seniors in their high-school graduating class
   d. the dates of employment for a recent job, preferably one at which they no longer work
   e. the ideal salary for a job offered them upon graduation and the ideal location of that job

3. Ask students to write sentences about three or four statistics found in an almanac or in *The Guinness Book of Records*.

ANSWERS TO EXERCISES

■ **Exercise 1** (p. 112)   **Striking out forms inappropriate in formal writing**

Inappropriate *forms which students should strike out are listed below.*

1. a dr.
2. in Calif. and Ill.
3. on Magnolia St.
4. on Aug. 15
5. for Jr.
6. before six in the A.M.

■ **Exercise 2** (p. 114)   **Using appropriate shortened forms**

1. on June 15 OR on June 15th
2. Dr. Ernest Threadgill OR Ernest Threadgill, M.D.
3. $30 million OR $30,000,000
4. Janine Keith, C.P.A.
5. 1 P.M. OR 1 p.m. OR 1:00 P.M. OR 1:00 p.m.
6. by December 1, 1985 OR by 1 December 1985
7. at the bottom of page 15
8. 400 B.C.
9. in act 1, scene 2 OR Act I, Scene 2
10. (1985–1990) OR (1985–90)

12
THE COMMA

To use commas conscientiously is to keep in mind the structure and the readability of the sentence. Effective writers place commas in order to separate and clarify elements of the sentence in accord with the patterns of English, thereby giving perspective to and showing relationships between the parts of the sentence. Effective writers know that knowledge of sentence structure and the ability to use commas correctly go together; they also know that the pauses signaled by commas should facilitate the reader's comprehension of ideas.

Commas separate elements, thus grouping and isolating on all levels: the level of word (*aggressive, articulate salesperson*—see **12c**), of phrase (*Janet's favorite pet, an Irish setter, requires frequent grooming*—see **12d**), and of clause (*She loves to read biographies of artists, but her favorite summer pastime is attending craft shows*—see **12a**). Commas even separate one level from another; for example, a sentence modifier is separated from the sentence by a comma (*Unfortunately, the class was canceled before we could register for it*). Because commas work within as well as between levels, it is useful to point out the difficulty in reading a sentence with too many—albeit correctly placed—commas:

> When Jean, humming and smiling mysteriously, entered the crowded, hushed waiting room, she saw two sullen children, a distraught parent, and a harried receptionist, who was retrieving scattered toys.

In this sentence the number of ideas obscures the major divisions of adverb clause and main clause. The commas do not cause the problem; they are an indication of it.

To help students see the problem, ask them for revisions to improve the readability of the sentence. Allow them to see that some rearrangements change the meaning. Although creating two sentences is one option, assure them that as long as the two major divisions are clearly marked, all of the ideas can remain in one sentence:

> Jean, humming and smiling mysteriously, entered the crowded, hushed waiting room; there she saw two sullen children, a distraught parent, and a harried receptionist, who was retrieving scattered toys.

Two tests help students identify coordinate adjectives. First, coordinate adjectives may be joined by *and:*

soggy, bedraggled puppy	OR	soggy and bedraggled puppy
	BUT NOT	
difficult biology exam		difficult and biology exam
crumpled typing paper		crumpled and typing paper

Second, coordinate adjectives may be reversed and still communicate the same meaning:

soggy, bedraggled puppy	OR	bedraggled, soggy puppy
	BUT NOT	
difficult biology exam		biology difficult exam
crumpled typing paper		typing crumpled paper
long wooden ladder		wooden long ladder

Note: When linking main clauses with coordinating conjunctions, students should be aware of the various meanings of these connectives:

and—in addition, also, moreover, besides
but OR **yet**—nevertheless, however, still
for—because, seeing that, since
or—as an alternative, otherwise
nor—and not, or not, not either   [used after a negative]
so—therefore, as a result

Advise students to consult the dictionary when they are in any doubt about the meaning of a connective. See also **3b** and **32c(4)**.

ACTIVITIES

1. Ask students to insert commas between main clauses separated by a co-ordinating conjunction:

   a. We raked the leaves into ten small piles but Jerry argued that three large piles would look better.
   b. I fertilized the garden and watered it thoroughly every week.
   c. Did you buy carpet for the kitchen floor or did you decide to wait until parquet flooring is on sale before you remodel the kitchen?
   d. They saved their money for a two-week vacation in New York but finally decided to rent a houseboat instead.
   e. Marlene did not want to wax her car nor did she want to pay someone else to do it.

2. Have students write sentences following the pattern *Adverb clause, main clause.* Then have students rewrite the sentences using the pattern *Main clause adverb clause.* Suggest as subordinators *as soon as, because, until, wherever,* and *provided;* or have students select from those listed on page 20.

3. To help students distinguish restrictive from nonrestrictive clauses, have them answer each of the following questions twice in complete sentences— the first with a restrictive clause, the second with a nonrestrictive clause.

   a. Who has helped you the most?

1. An instructor who explains rules clearly helps me become a better writer.
2. Professor Grimes, who always returns papers promptly, advised me to use subordination more often.

b. Who listens to your problems?
c. What job would you like to have upon graduation?
d. Which sibling do you most often compete with?
e. Who is one person you admire?

4. Before assigning Section **12**, have students select one body paragraph from a recent theme, copy every comma use, and give a reason for it. Suggest that students use a chart and that they be honest in listing their reasons:

Comma	Reason
went downstairs, he	comma after an introductory clause
claque, cleek, or *clique*	comma with items in a series
For example,	don't know; sounded good

Students' reasons may range from an honest "don't know" to the statement of a rule. When students have finished, collect the chart and the paragraph. After Section **12** has been taught, return the chart and the paragraph, asking students to correct the punctuation and then to make a justification chart for the revised paragraph. Have students compare the two charts and write a brief description of how their use of the comma has improved.

5. Ask students to explain the uses of the comma in one paragraph taken from one of their textbooks or a favorite magazine.

ANSWERS TO EXERCISES

Since punctuation is often a matter of individual preference, much of the key to exercises in Sections **12–17** should be considered as merely suggestive— indicative of one instructor's preferences.

■ **Exercise 1** (pp. 118–19)   **Linking sentences with *and, but, or, nor, for, so,* or *yet***

1. strikes**,** *and* another [OR *so* OR *and so*]
2. bars**,** *nor* did it make
3. immediately**,** *or* they may
4. vacation**,** *for* they needed
5. whistle**,** *but* she cannot

■ **Exercise 2** (p. 119)   **Inserting commas before connectives**

1. questionnaires, and they had
2. fill, for Bob
3. later, but I
4. movie, and the
5. party, but Gary

■ **Exercise 3** (p. 122)   **Punctuating adverb clauses and introductory phrases**

1. else, forget   6. √
2. know, these   7. sledgehammer, these
3. time, I OR time I   8. √
4. noon, the OR noon the   9. over, the
5. downhill, the   10. can, help

■ **Exercise 5** (p. 127)   **Using commas with nonrestrictive elements**

1. Mary Smith, who
2. √
3. Berry, sitting . . . window,
4. √
5. hometown, a little
6. √
7. *The Rivals*, a Mrs.
8. √
9. Falls, which . . . 1871, was
10. Duke, Jr., and

■ **Exercise 6** (pp. 128–29)   **Using commas with appositives, contrasted elements, and names, dates, and addresses**

1. bugs, not
2. Avenue, San Diego, CA
3. Sandpoint, Idaho,
4. Valentine, Nebraska, on January 7, not
5. November 14, 1984,

■ **Exercise 7** (pp. 130–31)   **Inserting needed commas**

1. When I was six, we moved closer to civilization,
2. It was a middle-class neighborhood, not a blackboard jungle; there was no war, no hunger, no racial strife.
3. My guess is that as the family breaks down, friendships
4. But alas, I do not rule the world and that, I am afraid, is the story of my life—always a godmother, never a God.
5. If all else fails, try
6. spring, a brilliant . . . September 22, 1979, in

7. Incidentally, supporting . . . expensive, some
8. drunkenness, nor
9. lived," said Mick Pattemore, his accent . . . Sweetwater, Texas, but Somerset, England
10. relationship, smooth

■ **Exercise 8** (p. 131)   **Class discussion of commas**

In sentence 3 commas could be inserted as follows:

> you, you [**12b**]
> realized, and [**12a**]
> it, the whole [**12b**]
> lashed up, squirming [**12d**]

In the closing sentence, rule **12d(3)** *can explain the parenthetical or appended elements.*

13
SUPERFLUOUS COMMAS

Once students have studied the rules in Section **12**, the result—usually for the next theme or two—is commas, commas everywhere. Even students who had no problems with the comma before tend to overcomma their prose until they can comfortably and correctly apply the rules that their style most often calls upon. By reemphasizing the comma's relationship to structure and readability, however, you can stem this flow.

Short introductory phrases and slightly parenthetical phrases (**13c**) become the objects of students' desire to separate elements. Introductory prepositional phrases are especially likely to be set off by commas if they contain more than three words (*In modern research laboratories*). To be realistic, such phrases are increasingly set off by commas, and often it is the writer who decides whether the comma is desirable. Frequently, students insert commas before the coordinating conjunction linking the elements of a compound subject or compound verb and even before the conjunction linking coordinate adjectives—either because they confuse these structures with coordinate main clauses or because they have simply formed the habit of using a comma before any coordinating conjunction.

Also, students try to improve readability by using a comma between the subject and verb in the belief that the comma helps the reader see the most important separation in the sentence. What they do not realize is that while English sentences are binary, the separation of subject and verb by a comma works against the completion of meaning, for once readers come upon the subject or the verb, they then search out the word(s) that complete the central thought.

ACTIVITIES

1. Ask students who make the errors discussed in Section **13** to complete a justification chart after they have made the necessary corrections in their themes.

2. Have students correct the misused commas in the following sentences. (See **13b**.)

   a. Beth makes lists of things to do, and plans her time efficiently.
   b. The most important tasks are at the top of the list, so, she concentrates on them first.
   c. Beth has learned to accomplish even more by delegating household chores to her children yet, she always reserves some time every evening for her hobbies.

d. Playing backgammon, or cross-country skiing are her winter favorites, but, during the summer she prefers racing hot-air balloons.

ANSWERS TO EXERCISES

■ **Exercise 1** (p. 134) **Explaining the absence of commas**

1. **13c**   3. **13b**   5. **13c**   7. **13b**
2. **13a**   4. **13d**   6. **13b**; **13c**

■ **Exercise 2** (pp. 134–35) **Changing sentences and deleting unneeded commas**

1. trees and pounded
2. facts and predicts
3. work and may
4. People who lead rather than demand often get good results.
5. A boy who is willing to work can get a job here.

■ **Exercise 3** (p. 135) **Circling superfluous commas**

1. are ⊙ at least ⊙ three
2. First ⊙ is
3. favorite ⊙ fishing . . . spot ⊙ where
4. fish ⊙ is . . . he ⊙ generally ⊙ gets
5. person ⊙ who
6. him ⊙ and . . . anything ⊙ fit . . . as ⊙ perch
7. bank ⊙ by
8. one ⊙ great . . . big ⊙ wad
   out ⊙ and . . . pole ⊙ so
9. Then ⊙ he
10. He ⊙ sometimes ⊙ dozes.
11. Also ⊙ he
12. CORRECT
13. CORRECT
14. line ⊙ and ⊙ to

14
THE SEMICOLON

A comparatively rare mark of punctuation, the semicolon clarifies the structure of the sentence and thus increases readability. As with the comma, correct use of the semicolon depends on students' mastery of sentence structure. Hence, beginning the study of the semicolon with a discussion of the phrase "parts of unequal grammatical rank" facilitates the study of this section and offers an opportunity to review phrases and clauses.

Levels of grammatical rank may be classified according to their ability to function as independent units of expression; from highest to lowest, the levels are sentence, main clause, subordinate clause, phrase (noun, verb, prepositional, gerund, infinitive, participial), word, and letter. Both a sentence and a main clause may function as independent units; however, a sentence ranks above a main clause because a sentence may include a number of main clauses (*They lived in Minneapolis until they retired; then they moved to Santa Barbara.*).

A semicolon separates parts of equal grammatical rank but not parts from two different ranks. It may, for example, separate two sentences or two clauses or a series of identical structures already containing commas. It does not, however, separate different types of phrases from each other, such as a noun phrase from a verb phrase or a participial phrase from a noun phrase.

ACTIVITIES

1. Ask students to tell whether or not the units in each item are of equal grammatical rank and to what rank each unit belongs.

   a. As soon as she spoke / because of her wit   [clause / phrase]
   b. She spoke with authority / when she delivered her speech   [sentence or main clause / subordinate clause]
   c. Phrasing her thoughts carefully / she measured the crowd's reaction while she spoke   [phrase / sentence]
   d. An articulate and calm speaker / a speaker of unsurpassed poise   [phrase / phrase]
   e. She spoke; they listened / she spoke while they listened   [sentence / sentence]
   f. Should have been listening attentively / as she replied   [phrase / clause]
   g. Offering the latest statistics, she refuted the argument that he gave / to have refuted it so effortlessly   [sentence / phrase]
   h. Since the proposal was defeated / her rational argument was accepted by even those who had been opposed at first   [clause / sentence]

i. According to the latest statistics / against the proposal   [phrase / phrase]

j. She knew she had won / she congratulated herself   [sentence / sentence or main clause]

2. Ask students to write two sentences for each pattern, punctuating the sentences as in the pattern.

   a. Subordinate clause, main clause; main clause subordinate clause.
   b. Main clause; transitional phrase, main clause.
   c. Main clause; main clause.
   d. Participial phrase, main clause subordinate clause; main clause.
   e. Main clause with items in a series; conjunctive adverb, main clause subordinate clause.

3. Have students collect five sentences containing semicolons and identify the rule for each use. Encourage students to locate sentences for both **14a** and **14b**. Ask students what they conclude about the use of semicolons, such as how often they are found; whether they more often illustrate rule **14a** or **14b**; and whether they are found more often in informal or formal writing.

4. Reinforce rule **14a** and relate it to use of the period (**17a**) by dictating pairs of ideas that could be written as one compound sentence or as two simple sentences. Ask students to decide whether a comma or a semicolon is better. It may also be useful to include some ideas that are apparently unrelated and refer students to **23a**.

ANSWERS TO EXERCISES

■ **Exercise 1** (pp. 138–39)   **Using semicolons between main clauses**

1. marriage; a family   [. . . *marriage, nor is a family quarrel a broken home* is also correct.]
2. use; for example,
3. spin-offs; from
4. self-defense; later,
5. blew up; as a result,

■ **Exercise 2** (p. 139)   **Using semicolons to separate items in a series**

1. advocate; K. C. Miles, a theologian; and . . .
2. comedians; experts . . . leaders; and authors . . .

■ **Exercise 3** (p. 140)   **Correcting misused semicolons**

1. afternoon, never
2. bore, at least
3. peeves, jokes OR peeves: jokes OR peeves—jokes
4. five minutes, the doors
5. charge, the OR charge—the

■ **Exercise on the comma and the semicolon** (pp. 141–42)

Optional commas are enclosed in parentheses.

1. courses, for
2. Felipe, a visiting professor from Kenya, says
3. fish, . . . rhubarb, . . . tomatoes, and
4. scrawny, mangy-looking
5. gear, and . . . firewood, I
6. wife, Jerry
7. Still(,) in high school(,) we . . . facts(,) such as 1066, the Battle of Has-
   tings; 1914–1918, World War I; 1939–1945, World War II; and 1969, the
   first
8. Rockies; to tell the truth, however, they
9. mercy; his victim(,) for justice
10. end; however, my

15

THE APOSTROPHE

Of the three uses of the apostrophe, the possessive case of nouns and indefinite pronouns causes students the most trouble. First they must recognize the situations that require the possessive and then work out a method for affixing its sign. Since the possessive case signals more than ownership alone, students may not recognize all of the occasions that call for it. In *An Introductory English Grammar,* 2nd ed. (New York: Holt, 1971) 127–28, Norman C. Stageberg lists six relationships that are signaled (the examples here are similar to those Stageberg uses):

possession	David's videorecorder
description or characterization	driver's license
origin	Dillard's prose
measure—time	a day's time
—value	two cents' worth
—space	at arm's length
subject of act	Steve's regret; he regrets
object of act	Mary Ann's captors; someone captured her

But knowing when to use the possessive does not guarantee knowing how to use it. Many a student has avoided deciding *'s* or *s'* by writing the apostrophe above the *s,* thus suggesting that in the haste of getting down the idea the student intended the correct placement but failed (and students smile knowingly when the instructor says that this subterfuge is not unfamiliar). Students can follow a three-step process to select the correct form. First, they decide the word; second, they decide the number; third, they decide the sign of possession, as in these examples:

dean	(sing.) dean	**15a(1)** dean's
woman	(pl.) women	**15a(2)** women's
Richards	(pl.) Richardses	**15a(2)** Richardses'
sheep	(sing.) sheep	**15a(2)** sheep's
Secretary of State	(pl) Secretaries of State	**15a(3)** Secretaries of State's

Thus, rather than confronting number and possession simultaneously, students learn to determine number first and spell plurals correctly before affixing the sign of possession.

Finally, knowing how to use possessive forms requires students to distinguish between personal and indefinite pronouns, for indefinite pronouns take *'s* but personal pronouns do not. After all, they may think, a pronoun is a pronoun and possessive is possessive, so the possessive forms of *anybody* and *it* are *anybody's* and *it's.* A review of indefinite and personal pronouns may be necessary, or if the only troublesome form is *its*, then distinguishing between the possessive and the contraction may be sufficient; in fact, you may wish simply to point out that *its* corresponds in form to *hers* and *his*.

ACTIVITIES

1. If necessary, have students review **18d(5)** (forming the plural of nouns). Then ask them to write the singular and plural possessive forms for each of the following:

chemist	chemist's	chemists'
class	class's OR class' (depending on context)	classes'
committee	committee's	committees'
Elk City	Elk City's	Elk Citys'
fox	fox's	foxes'
beach	beach's	beaches'
staff	staff's	staffs' OR staves'
volcano	volcano's	volcano(e)s'
cactus	cactus's OR cactus'	cacti's OR cactuses'
member-at-large	member-at-large's	members-at-large's
people	people's	peoples'
other	other's	others'

Ask students for which, if any, they would use *of* instead of *'s* (such as the votes of the two members-at-large or the ceremony honoring the mayors of the two Elk Citys). Also single out *each other* and *one another* for discussion: although plural in meaning, the possessive forms are *each others'* and *one another's*. Ask the class to distinguish differences in meaning shown by *other's, others',* and *others*.

2. Have students supply the two forms that correspond to the one already supplied, rewording as necessary.

     EXAMPLE   It is <u>Nancy's</u> gift; her gift; hers.

     a. It is _____ car (*their*).
     b. I ordered _____ dinners (*Ethan's and my*).
     c. This racquet belongs to _____ (*you*).
     d. The camper is _____ (*his*).
     e. _____ favorite color is yellow (*Frances's*).

3. Have students write these sentences as they are being dictated.

     I wonder whose essay was typed on graph paper. Whether it's hers or his makes no difference. This paper with its fine lines makes reading difficult. Who's going to argue that it's acceptable manuscript form?

ANSWERS TO EXERCISES

■ **Exercise 1** (p. 145)   **Using apostrophes to indicate the possessive case**

1. John L. Field III's acreage
2. the Weinsteins' boat
3. Bess's (OR Bess') and Mary's voices
4. the editor-in-chief's efforts
5. Doris's (OR Doris') strategy
6. a quarter's worth
7. somebody else's ideas
8. Dickens' stories OR Dickens's stories
9. women's shoes
10. Henry and Ross' song OR Henry and Ross's song OR Henry's and Ross' song OR Henry's and Ross's song

■ **Exercise 2** (p. 146)   **Using apostrophes correctly**

1. students' (Option: 1980's)
2. Hughes' (Option: Hughes's)
3. Ross's
4. They're
5. '90; Jerry's
6. It's; C.P.A.'s; isn't
7. *i*'s; *s*'s
8. There's
9. OPEC's
10. else's

16
QUOTATION MARKS

Sections **16a**, **b**, and **e** contain information students will use as they write their research papers. For that reason, this section (along with **17i** on ellipsis points) can be logically included in the part of the course devoted to the research paper. Emphasis should be placed on accurate quotation as well as accurate punctuation since the respect given a piece of writing is at least in part a result of its author's respect for others' material.

As students look at a passage, they should ask: What is the controlling idea of this passage? How is the controlling idea related to the ideas in my paper? Does it support my ideas? What point does it support or illustrate? What are the two or three key phrases? Do the phrases merit direct quotation? If so, how can they be integrated into my own sentence? Would my use of the ideas be as effective if they were summarized or paraphrased? (See **34c** in the handbook and p. 117 of Section **34** of the *Instructor's Manual.*)

Students who learn how to evaluate sources in this fashion are more easily convinced that other sources should support their ideas, not replace them; writers who have something they think worth saying will not want too many or overly long quotations robbing them of that opportunity. At the same time, they do not risk losing their reader's patience (students often admit that as soon as they see a long prose quotation, they decide not to read it).

The following example shows the successive embedding indicated by the alternation of double and single quotation marks:

Original source
Few can read Mark Bradley's "Chronicles of a 'Suburban Rookie' at the Annual Block Party" without giggling, chortling, or roaring at the essayist's collection of neighborhood types.   —ELIZABETH COOKE

Sentence in a research paper
Readers of Bradley's essay can hardly think of suburbanites as dull, for "few can read . . .'Chronicles of a "Suburban Rookie" at the Annual Block Party' without giggling, chortling, or roaring at the essayist's collection of neighborhood types." (Cooke 110)

Although students rarely need all three levels, they should know that a method exists for handling the situation when it arises.

A more common problem is the overuse of quotation marks for slang or colloquial words. In an attempt to demonstrate their recognition that the word does not fit the rest of the prose, students add quotation marks rather than revise. However, occasionally a slang word may be appropriate, or have no synonym in general English. *Wimp* is such a word. Not yet in any dictionary, its only synonym is *milquetoast,* which presents the same difficulty since it is perceived as quaint. Attempts at irony, humor, or cleverness deserve attention. Students may have little awareness of irony, and still less experience conveying it in writing, so they will benefit from your analysis of the reasons for the misused quotation marks and some suggestions for more effective ways to convey ideas. It is rare that students use quotation marks for emphasis; however, instructors may wish to raise the point, particularly if some students do use them.

ACTIVITIES

1. Ask students to identify direct and indirect quotations and to punctuate the sentences.

   a. She wondered why she had agreed to babysit the twins
   b. Have I forgotten what they did the last time she mused
   c. Well she sighed at least they can't have any more mining expeditions in the backyard their shovels mysteriously disappeared
   d. She had forgotten to ask whether their batons had also been confiscated since her last visit
   e. Perhaps I just don't remember she declared how mischievous two little girls can be

2. Ask students to gather five sentences on a topic of their choice (language, marriage, heroes, success, philosophy, and so on). Then have them write sentences that quote the passages they have collected and ask them to provide documentation.

3. Ask students to write down an actual conversation. To concentrate on recording what is said, the students should not take part in the conversation; an overheard conversation or some radio or television dialogue works well. Once the dialogue is on paper, the students should add appropriate punctuation marks and dialogue tags.

4. Using an essay to which all students have access, write a series of quotations which students are to check for accuracy. Include an error in spelling, an omitted word, an omitted single quotation mark, omitted double quotation marks, transposed words, improper capitalization, and so on. Select different sentences for each error, and include two or three accurate sentences in the exercise.

5. Ask students to follow **16a(3)** as they quote one passage of prose or poetry that appeals to them.

ANSWERS TO EXERCISES

■ **Exercise 1** (pp. 150–51)   **Punctuating direct and indirect quotations**

Sentences containing indirect quotations may vary somewhat. Tense may vary in direct quotations.

1. Doris said, "I have a theory about you."
2. He said, "I have read David Baltimore's 'The Brain of a Cell'."
3. A Weight Watcher, Eileen explained, "I can eat as much as I want—of vegetables like spinach, eggplant, and zucchini."
4. Clyde asked whether I would go to the opera with him.
5. Last night Pruett said, "I think that Amanda's favorite expression is 'Tell me about it!'"

■ **Exercise 2** (p. 152)   **Using quotation marks correctly**

1. "Cloning,"
2. "stoked" means "fantastically happy on a surfboard." (Option: italics instead of quotation marks)
3. "A Circle in the Fire."
4. "Sighting the Target."
5. "My grandmother often said, 'When poverty comes in the door, love goes out the window.'"

■ **Exercise 3** (p. 154)   **Inserting needed quotation marks**

1. "The Star-Spangled Banner"?
2. "Get aholt," instead of "get hold,"
3. "I Just Called to Say I Love You."
4. "The Road Not Taken."
5. "No," Peg said, "I didn't . . . bananas yet!"
6. "Why I Want a Wife"?
7. "Miss Ellie Comes Home,"
8. "First Confession"; mine is "A Rose for Emily."
9. "Why cry over spilled milk?" my grandmother used to ask. "Be glad . . . to spill."
10. Catherine said, "Do the townspeople ever say to me 'You're a born leader'? Yes, lots of times, and when they do, I just tell them my motto is 'Lead, follow, or get the heck out of the way'!" OR . . . out of the way!'"

17

THE PERIOD AND OTHER MARKS

The literal meaning of *punctuate* is "to mark with a point." Inexperienced writers, faced with a number of marks to signal intonation patterns and the relative importance of ideas within sentences, may simply ignore them, preferring to use the dash for all internal punctuation and the period for the end of every sentence. Experienced writers, however, understand that observing the proprieties of punctuation enables them to communicate more effectively than relying on one or two marks to make all the distinctions of nine.

Punctuation exercises and activities give students not only practice with individual marks but also awareness of the options and distinctions available for a single instance. As a result, they learn that they can communicate meaning through punctuation as well as through diction and word arrangement.

Note that **17a(2)** lists *all* of the abbreviations which require a period. Also, MLA has adopted the standard postal abbreviations for states—without periods. Notice also that the key to rule **17e(3)** is the combination of *introductory* and *list*. Not all lists are followed by dashes, nor are all introductory series.

ACTIVITIES

1. Ask students to write sentences with the following information, first using a colon and then a dash. Example: *Three famous women who never married are Elizabeth Blackwell, Maria Montessori, and Emily Dickinson.* (*Book of Lists* 278)

   > Marriage is not a prerequisite of success: the careers of Elizabeth Blackwell, Maria Montessori, and Emily Dickinson show that a woman is not successful in her job because she is married.

   > Elizabeth Blackwell, Maria Montessori, Emily Dickinson—these are famous women who never married.

   a. The three most landed-on spaces in Monopoly are Illinois Avenue, Go, and B. & O. Railroad (*Book of Lists* 375).
   b. Three benefits of regular exercise are improved body tone, increased endurance, and increased self-respect.
   c. Three words beginning with *dh* are *dhak, dharma,* and *dhole.*
   d. Three famous American writers who married are Nathaniel Hawthorne, F. Scott Fitzgerald, and Robert Frost.
   e. Three U.S. Presidents whose birthdays occur in March are Andrew Jackson, John Tyler, and Grover Cleveland.
   f. Nicknames for *Mary* are *Mamie, May, Molly,* and *Polly.*

2. Have students compose sentences to illustrate each of the following:

    a. a direct question
    b. an indirect question
    c. a double direct question
    d. a direct quotation containing an indirect question
    e. question marks between parts of a series

3. *Parentheses* comes from the Greek *parentithenai,* meaning "a putting in beside," and this exactly describes the act of interpolating material that is independent from the syntax of the sentence but that qualifies the ideas in it. Parenthetical information is apart from yet related to. A writer must decide how much emphasis the parenthetical information should receive and then use the corresponding punctuation mark. Dashes emphasize most strongly, parentheses less so, and commas (because they are the most common of the three) least. Have students discuss the effect of the punctuation in each sentence:

    a. No one—not even his mother—recognized him after he had lost seventy pounds.
    b. No one (not even his mother) recognized him after he had lost seventy pounds.
    c. No one, not even his mother, recognized him after he had lost seventy pounds.

Ask them how the punctuation marks in each sentence reflect the writer's attitude toward the weight loss and other people's reaction to it.

4. Lists enumerated within a sentence are separated by commas and the numbers are enclosed in parentheses. Lists in vertical columns use numbers followed by a period:

> In deciding whether to quote from a source, a writer considers (1) the authority of the writer, (2) the relationship of the passage to the thesis of the research paper, and (3) the function of the passage in the research paper.

> In deciding whether to quote from a source, a writer considers
> 1. the authority of the writer
> 2. the relationship of the passage to the thesis of the research paper
> 3. the function of the passage in the research paper.

Have students enumerate the courses required for their major field of study, the arguments for a career in their major field of study, the arguments against a career in that field, and five questions to ask when considering a career in that field.

5. Following the structure of Exercise 5 (p. 167), use passages from several related articles (perhaps those in the students' anthology of essays) and ask students to quote according to instructions. Or use one passage reproduced on an overhead transparency and highlight the words to be omitted. Ask students to write a direct quotation omitting the words you specify.

6. Ask students to collect one or two examples of sentences punctuated according to **17a**, **17e**, **17f**, **17h**, and **17i** (one or two illustrations of each).

7. Have students use the punctuation marks in this chapter as they revise one or two paragraphs from their themes. Then ask them to select what they think are three major punctuation revisions and explain what was gained by each.

ANSWERS TO EXERCISES

■ **Exerise 2** (p. 160)   **Adding colons**

1. 12:30; quotation:
2. √
3. these:
4. periodicals:
5. √

■ **Exercise 3** (p. 160)   **Using semicolons or colons between main clauses**

1. purpose: 3. certain;
2. purpose;   4. certain:

■ **Exercise 4** (p. 164)   **Punctuating parenthetical elements**

Punctuation setting off parenthetical matter may vary.

1. Gibbs—or is it his twin brother?—plays
2. Joseph, who is Gordon's brother, is
3. "I admit that I—" he began
4. everything—more
5. courses—for example, French and biology—demand
6. Silverheels (1918–1980) played
7. fool [sic] the
8. Body language—a wink or yawn, nose-rubbing or ear pulling, folded arms or crossed legs—can . . .
9. lakes—these
10. innovations—for example, the pass/fail system—did not

■ **Exercise 5** (p. 167)   **Using the ellipsis mark**

According to John Donne, "No man is an island . . . every man is a piece of the continent, a part of the main. . . . Any man's death diminishes me because I am involved in mankind."

■ **Exercise 6** (p. 167)   **Using the ellipsis mark**

1. My father was dying **. . .** what would happen to us?
2. Our lives would have been different if **. . . .**

■ **Exercise 7** (pp. 167–68)   **Using end marks, commas, colons, dashes, and parentheses**

Answers may vary somewhat.

1. same: aluminum guardrails, green signs, white lettering.
2. "Is it—is it the green light then?" was all I managed to say.
3. again: What . . . theater.
4. typo: "The . . . refugees."
5. "Judy!" she exploded. "Judy, that's . . . say."
   She raised . . . daughter, but it wouldn't reach.
6. Emily (formerly Mrs. Goyette) caught . . . urgently.
7. wished to be—a professional dancer.
8. thinkers—conservatives or liberals—who . . . human.
9. put it, "Rose Bowl, Sugar Bowl, and Orange Bowl—all are gravy bowls."
10. "very" ("I am good and mad"), and . . . coffee, not the cup, is hot.

18

SPELLING AND HYPHENATION

Because spelling problems vary from student to student, no one approach to teaching spelling will help all students uniformly, but the suggestions that begin Section **18** are sound advice to all writers. Whenever possible, instruction in spelling should be individualized to meet the needs of the class or, ideally, of each student.

One method is to compile a list of the three or four most frequently misspelled words in a set of themes and to present the words with appropriate spelling rules in the process of returning the themes. Working from students' writing, you are then sure to teach the words that need attending to rather than dwelling on words that cause the class little problem. Further, over the semester you might want to compile a class list; the words that recur in more than two sets of themes could be assigned for special study.

A second approach is to have students keep a list of words which they have misspelled in their writing. Rather than ask students to recopy the misspelling (which reinforces the error), have them write down the correct spelling and the rule or device which will help them remember the spelling. Such a list might look like this:

An Individual Spelling List

---

laid—like *said*	[analogy]
forfeit—not an *ee* sound	[rule reference]
minor—minority	[change of stress]
category—cat-e-gory	[syllabication]
recommend—re + commend	[structural analysis]
studying—y + ing	[rule reference]
together—to get her	[mnemonic device]
accept—to accept gifts	[use in context]

Spelling can be tested in a number of ways. Here are some suggestions:

1. Assign groups of twenty words a week chosen from the list of frequently misspelled words plus those on the class list; then dictate ten of them for the students to write down. This approach has the advantage of being quick, easy, and familiar; and students have said that it causes them to be more careful with all spellings as they prepare an essay.
2. Give each student several words to spell orally.
3. To test easily confused words, dictate words in context and ask students to write either the word or the phrase.
4. Ask students to write a paragraph using selected words.

5. Write a multiple-choice quiz, asking students to select the one mis-spelled word from a series of three to five words, or the one correctly spelled word from a series of misspelled words.

In short, spelling is a skill that students who want their ideas to be taken seri-ously must master, but testing spelling need not be limited to a single method.

For **18d** two cautions are in order. First, students should realize that not all words ending in *f* or *fe* change the ending to *ve* before adding *s* (*safes, proofs, beliefs, handkerchiefs*); some have two plural forms (*hoofs, hooves; scarfs, scarves*). Second, they should realize that *-es* (not *-s*) marks the plural in such words as *tomatoes* and *potatoes;* thus, *tomatoe* and *potatoe* are incorrect sin-gular forms.

ACTIVITIES

1. Have students pronounce correctly each word listed in **18a**. Ask students what mispronunciation they hear in the speech of others (not, of course, in their speech or that of their classmates). Some frequent mispronunciations are

disastrous	pertain	relevant
escape	prescribe	recognize
everything	probable	quantity or quantity

2. Have students choose the correct forms:

    a. If you expect to (*accept, except*) their dinner invitation, I'd (*advice, advise*) you to (*choose, chose*) some loosely fitting (*clothes, cloths*).

    b. They usually serve five or six (*coarses, courses*) (*altogether, all to-gether*), and the table setting (*always, all ways*) (*complements, compli-ments*) the food. Not even the diet-(*conscience, conscious*) are unim-pressed by the (*desert, dessert*)—raspberry torte.

    c. (*Sense, Since*) you can do no better (*than, then*) to dine in the (*pres-ence, presents*) of such (*holy, wholly*) gracious hosts, my (*council, counsel*) is to (*precede, proceed*) with your plans to attend what (*maybe, may be*) a (*lessen, lesson*) in attention to every (*miner, minor*) detail.

    d. Use (*your, you're*) best (*stationary, stationery*) to (*rite, write, right*) a thank-you note; a genuine (*complement, compliment*) (*formerly, for-mally*) given is (*all ways, always*) welcome.

3. Ask students to use hyphenated words as adjectives in listing five qualities that describe their ideal spouse (such as *bluegrass-loving cowboy, well-groomed botanist, a wife with a one-day-at-a-time philosophy of life*). Also ask students to use five *-ly*-adverb-adjective combinations to describe their ideal instructor (*basically optimistic adult, totally organized lecturer*).

ANSWERS TO EXERCISES

■ **Exercise 1** (pp. 175–76)   **Adding suffixes**

1. likely, safely, surely
2. excitable, exciting, excitement
3. coming, noticing, hoping
4. using, useless
5. continuous, courageous
6. careful, hopeful, useful
7. arguing, argument, arguable
8. completely, completing
9. desirable, noticeable
10. managing, management

■ **Exercise 2** (p. 176)   **Forming present participles and past tense**

1. admitting, admitted
2. bragging, bragged
3. concealing, concealed
4. gripping, gripped
5. hoping, hoped
6. jogging, jogged
7. planning, planned
8. rebelling, rebelled
9. stopping, stopped
10. auditing, audited

■ **Exercise 3** (p. 177)   **Adding suffixes**

1. variable, pliable
2. funnier, carrier
3. various, luxurious
4. easily, finally
5. supplied, stayed
6. studying, worrying
7. paid, laid
8. livelihood, likelihood
9. friendliness, loneliness
10. usually, coolly

■ **Exercise 4** (p. 178)   **Forming plurals**

1. beliefs
2. theories
3. churches
4. geniuses [RARE: genii for "spirits"]
5. Kellys
6. baths
7. heroes
8. stories
9. wishes
10. forties
11. radiuses OR radii
12. scarves OR scarfs
13. wives
14. speeches
15. tomatoes
16. phenomena OR phenomenons

17. halos OR haloes
18. children
19. handfuls
20. rodeos

■ **Exercise 5** (p. 179)   **Spelling with *ei* and *ie***

1. piece	6. apiece	11. niece
2. achieve	7. belief	12. shield
3. receive	8. conceive	13. weird
4. neigh	9. their	14. shriek
5. freight	10. deceit	15. priest

■ **Exercise 6** (p. 186)   **Using the hyphen**

1. a six-room house
2. people-eating sharks
3. ink-stained fingers
4. two-year-old cheese
5. cat-loving person
6. twenty-dollar books
7. all-night vigils
8. problem-solving parents
9. lily-covered pond
10. two-lane highway

■ **Exercise 7** (p. 187)   **Using needed hyphens**

1. self-respect
2. cigar-smoking men
3. sugar-cured ham
4. a nightlatch
5. V-shaped
6. all-purpose wax
7. snow-covered streets
8. Nome–L.A. flight OR Nome-to-L.A. flight
9. one-or-two-day sale
10. fifteen-year-old cars

19

GOOD USAGE AND GLOSSARY

A common misconception about dictionaries offers a good starting point for discussion of dictionary-making and attitudes toward language: *A modern dictionary tells us how words should be used.* Ask students what they understand *should be used* to mean. Then, ask students to give an example of a word that they think a dictionary will say is incorrect usage. Someone will undoubtedly mention *ain't.* Have students look the word up in three standard college dictionaries. (*American Heritage, Webster's New Collegiate,* and *Webster's New World* will probably be represented among the dictionaries students should bring to class that day. However, to insure that those dictionaries are represented, instructors may wish to bring them.) Have students read the usage note for *ain't* from each dictionary. They may be surprised to learn that whereas the *American Heritage Dictionary* labels *ain't Nonstandard* (followed by a long explanatory usage note) and *Webster's New Collegiate* labels it *Substandard, Webster's New World* accepts *ain't* as *Colloquial* for *am not.* Such an activity helps to break down the students' view of a dictionary as the authority on words and to point out that many dictionaries are descriptive rather than prescriptive. (Instructors may find it useful to explain the distinction.)

This is the time to give attention to the usage terms dictionaries use. When students are aware that lexicographers do not always agree about which usage label, if any, to give a word, they are ready to confront the differences in meaning among such terms as *Colloquial, Regional,* and *Informal.* Have students note the usage labels employed by their dictionaries. For example, the *American Heritage Dictionary* lists the following labels (pp. xlvi–xlvii):

1. *nonstandard*—for words not considered part of "standard, educated speech"
2. *informal*—for words "acceptable in conversation . . . [but] not . . . suitable in formal writing"
3. *slang*—for informal, usually short-lived, words whose aim is "to produce rhetorical effect, such as incongruity, irreverence, or exaggeration"
4. *vulgar*—for taboo words
5. *obsolete*—for words "no longer used except in quotation or intentional archaism"
6. *archaic*—for words "that once were common, but are currently rare and are readily identifiable as belonging to a style of language no longer in general use"
7. *rare*—for words used infrequently because their synonyms are used instead
8. *poetic*—for words common to poetry but not to prose
9. *regional*—for words used by or associated with one particular area

As an introduction to a few basic principles of language study, such assumptions as the following give beginning writers perspective on language:

1. Language is symbolic.
2. Living languages change.
3. Language has system.
4. Language has hierarchies (sound, syllable, word, sentence, paragraph).
5. Speech, not writing, is primary; writing is the graphic representation of sounds.

For a discussion of common but incorrect notions about language, see "Facts, Assumptions, and Misconceptions About Language," Chapter 1 of Thomas Pyles' and John Algeo's *The Origins and Development of the English Language,* 3rd ed. (New York: Harcourt, 1982).

ACTIVITIES

1. This list is a supplement to Exercise 5. Have students give the etymology of each of the following words:

a. aloof	h. turnpike	o. lieutenant
b. cereal	i. tuxedo	p. meander
c. gargle	j. tycoon	q. suede
d. grape	k. cartel	r. vinegar
e. laser	l. dollar	s. wacky
f. sideburns	m. glamour	t. zoo
g. telethon	n. gossip	

2. Have students use their dictionaries to identify the languages from which each of the following words was borrowed:

a. bungalow	e. judo	h. taboo
b. chocolate	f. mosquito	i. yam
c. flamboyant	g. succotash	j. yogurt
d. gruff		

3. Ask students to mark the root and the prefix or suffix of each word; then have students use the root and another affix to form a word:

a. underground	e. interlock	h. circumvent
b. admit	f. creative	i. vision
c. converse	g. judgment	j. propel
d. bisect		

4. Give students an opportunity to compare dictionaries while they learn about the kinds of information dictionaries contain. Have each student bring a standard college dictionary to class. Begin the class by asking for

the name of each dictionary and listing the titles on the chalkboard. Then ask students to help list the kinds of information contained in an entry: spelling, syllabication, pronunciation, stress, variant spellings, variant pronunciations, abbreviations, inflected forms, etymology, definitions (ordered by most common meaning or by historical order), part(s) of speech, usage label, examples of the word in context, synonyms, antonyms, usage notes. Shift attention from the entry to the entire dictionary by asking if the dictionaries contain the following and if so, where:

> abbreviations
> foreign terms
> geographical names
> population figures
> male and female first names
> names of famous people
> names and locations of U.S. colleges and universities
> charts of weights and measures
> illustrations
> forms of address in letters to public figures
> a history of English
> a chart of Indo-European and non-Indo-European languages
> a glossary or usage labels
> a chart of pronunciation symbols [Call attention to differences in the use of symbols by asking students for the symbols of the sounds italicized here: *th*ing, *sh*arp, *j*ustify, *fa*ther, *a*sk, and *u*rge.]

5. As a class activity, have students consult their dictionaries for

   a. the preferred pronunciations of *aunt, creek, exquisite, harass*
   b. the plurals of *criterion, elk, parenthesis, voodoo*
   c. the number of meanings for *in, plastic,* and *run* (verb)
   d. the usage label, if any, for *bib and tucker, keckle, once-over, potlatch, you-all, yummy*
   e. the parts of speech for *best, but, while*

6. To help students understand that dictionaries do not always agree even about spelling and that sometimes two spellings are equally correct, have students consult three dictionaries for the correct spelling(s) of the following words:

   a. focused   b. programed   c. alright

7. Using the dialect survey in Roger W. Shuy's *Discovering American Dialects* (NCTE, 1967), have students identify their speech and discuss why it is more difficult to define their dialects than those of their grandparents' time. Ask whether they think regional varieties of English will disappear.

8. Have students collect examples of jargon or gobbledygook and, for one

example, provide a translation in plain English. The two examples here illustrate the kind of language students should look for:

a. Rarely have I known, hither-to, the unalloyed pleasure of being the recipient of so concentrated a demonstration of domestic felicity as was lavished upon this unsuspecting beneficiary of your matchless hospitality. Truly, your hearth is a lodestone for the weary wayfarer, and your threshold an entrance to unimaginable delights.

—a Hallmark thank-you card

b.   Walking through the Soils Building at the University of Wisconsin in Madison, I stopped in front of a display case containing unusual soil and mineral specimens. One descriptive card read:

"Structure built by an avian engineer using solid waste (plastic, paper, tin foil); organic debris from vegetation; and mineral soil. The soil was compacted into a platy, stratified deposit which is essentially a series of crusts of reduced hydraulic conductivity. The structure, a segment of a concretion, is formed on a tree branch close to the canopy. It is an epiphytic pedological feature, whose fate is to be translocated by free fall to the soil surface, where it will eventually be incorporated into the soil, except that part which decomposes first."

Displayed in the glass case was a robin's nest.

—READER'S DIGEST

9. Have students write down a simple, brief sentence or familiar saying. Then ask them to translate it into jargon or gobbledygook. Ask students to read their jargon-sentence for others to decipher.

10. Ask students to compile examples of jargon used by one group (such as CB owners, grocery clerks, fast-food employees, computer programmers, pilots, or sailors) and to write a paragraph using as much of that jargon as possible.

11. Have students revise the following sentences according to the usage recommended in the **Glossary of Usage**.

a. All the farther I had yet to drive seems to be alot since I had already driven four hundred miles that day.

b. Its an awful long ways from South Dakota to Pennsylvania, especially on these kind of roads, when you're kinda tired plus you're suppose to be there before dinner time because your folks are waiting on you.

c. Be sure and stop in Milwaukee if you're fixing to have a fun vacation.

d. Hopefully, it's okay to show up unannounced if the visit's just only for a couple of hours.

e. No amount of coaxing will make me liable to accept an itinerary that's different than the one Lee and myself planned. The reason is because the perfect vacation is an allusion alright, but each and every summer the affects of all them glossy summer-vacation brochures gets us to making plans for a trip superior than last year's.

ANSWERS TO EXERCISES

No answers are given for the dictionary exercises in this section, as answers will vary according to the dictionary used.

■ **Exercise 9** (p. 201)   **Rewriting to eliminate jargon**

1. We have a good plan for success.
2. Don't open these doors.
3. We will discuss with the client ways to get more ads on the air.
4. Muzak makes people feel comfortable.
5. We discouraged thieves.

20
EXACTNESS

Students frequently have difficulty distinguishing between denotation and connotation. Rather than saying that denotation is the dictionary definition (dictionaries frequently include connotations in the definitions of words), try having students arrive at the concept empirically. For example, write the word *Thanksgiving* on the chalkboard and ask students to suggest words or phrases to define it. Some of the suggestions will be denotations: national holiday, day for giving thanks. Other suggestions will be connotations: turkeys, huge meals, family get-togethers, pumpkin pies, and so forth. Ask students to list all the denotations in one column and all the connotations in another. Any number of words can be treated in this manner until students are comfortable with the two concepts. Some useful words are those for family members and other loved ones (grandmother, boyfriend, best friend), prized possessions (automobile, house, other items of value), authority figures (coach, police officer, Dean of Men/Women/Students).

Students also are often mystified by advice to make their writing specific and concrete. After working through examples of abstract and specific language, it is helpful to caution students that excessive detail can interfere with their writing just as much as abstraction can (see **23b**). Some instructors may also wish to look ahead to the sections on the paragraph (Section **32**, particularly **32a**) and the whole composition (Section **33**, particularly **33c**) so students recognize that exact diction serves a rhetorical purpose. In particular, students might be asked to consider that a writer must transfer ideas from his or her mind to that of a reader and that this difficult task must be done with no immediate opportunity for the reader to ask questions about what the writer has said. And if that were not enough, consider some other possible obstacles:

1. uncertainty about what to say or how to say it
2. unconventional use of words, either because of errors in grammar or usage or because of an overly personalized language
3. a complex message
4. an audience hostile to prose and/or to the subject
5. audience distractions (television, the smell of food, conversation, a fire siren)
6. the differences between writer and audience in values, background, education, and experience
7. an audience using definitions of key words different from the writer's

Conscientious writers assume two things: first, that the message and the audience must both be considered and second, that if readers can misread or misunderstand, they will (sometimes going so far as to lose the meaning entirely). The choice of exact words is one important method for increasing the likelihood of the message's being interpreted as the writer conceived it.

The use of figurative language is another method by which writers make meaning exact. Metaphors and similes clarify the nature of something unknown or unfamiliar by comparing it to something familiar. For example, in "his tightly knit prose" the metaphor compares the intricacies of two structures: the securely intertwined loops of a sweater (the familiar) and the coherence of the author's writing (unfamiliar); the structure of both results from the pattern of connections.

Students, however, frequently have difficulty handling figurative language well either because they don't know how to integrate it with their ideas or because, recognizing the value instructors place on such language, they want to please. They can usually benefit from specific advice about using metaphors, similes, and personification: Does the metaphor (simile, personification) make the idea clearer? Is it consistent with the tone and approach of the essay?

Often defined as *figurative language gone stale,* clichés are sometimes useful, particularly when they can be turned to the writer's advantage—as many professional writers use them. However, students are well advised to be alert for clichés in their writing and to be sure that if they do use a cliché, they have not simply employed it as a kind of formula.

Like clichés, allusions can help writers achieve exactness. However, also like clichés, they should be used only with deliberation. The purpose of linking familiar phrases from literature or the Bible with the writer's idea is to make a point or connect ideas in a way no other words or references could. Such citations are valuable only if the audience recognizes them and understands how they make the writer's meaning exact. For example, the sentence "Apparently believing that his sound and fury signified something, the incensed customer continued his harangue" contains a reference to Macbeth's words, but the reader must recognize the allusion and the difference between the original speech and the words in this sentence in order to understand the irony of the man's continuing harangue. Of course, allusions used to pad ideas or to show off the writer's background should not be included.

ACTIVITIES

1. To make vivid the point that a variety of interpretations of a given word are possible, ask students to close their eyes (but to stay awake) and to listen to the next word or phrase spoken. After the instructor says the word *dog,* students should describe what they pictured when the word was said. The instructor should ask questions to help students describe the image precisely (breed, size, color, age, name, stance). Repeat the exercise using *tree* and then *gates of heaven* to illustrate the range of experiences and backgrounds that color the images of what are perceived as simple words.

2. On the chalkboard write this sentence: *Lynn walked into the room.* Give students a few seconds to think of several synonyms for *walk* and then call on every student (row by row) for a word to add to the list. Collecting forty or more words provides ample opportunity to discuss connotation. The exercise may be repeated by collecting synonyms for *said* or by asking

males to list synonyms for *female* and females to list synonyms for *male*. The latter exercise leads naturally into a discussion of what the various connotations suggest about how the sexes view each other.

3. Have students identify the similes, metaphors, or personifications in the following sentences and comment on the effectiveness of each:

   a. "Nina Brett's laugh was like tiny ice cubes falling into a thin glass from a great height." —GAIL GODWIN, *Glass People*

   b. "Like any encyclopedia, a great cathedral cannot be read at a glance. If one's time is limited, it is best to concentrate on a few particularly glorious chapters. At Bourges, these are the center portal of the west facade and the windows. These should be read slowly, with the aid of good binoculars." —*NEW YORK TIMES,* 19 Apr. 1981

   c. "A man and a woman . . . were staring up at a large black-and-white photograph of the great galaxy of Andromeda, a pinwheel of billions of stars that . . . was similar to our galaxy. . . ."
   —*NEW YORK TIMES,* 19 Apr. 1981

   d. "Such words and phrases [politicians' coinages] are but the insects of a season at the most." —GEORGE CAMPBELL, *The Philosophy of Rhetoric*

   e. " . . . the remarkable boundary between the lush green of the land blessed by the Nile's water and the barren, brown desert beyond the reach of irrigation. So clear and absolute is this line that from the air it looks as if a child has put down his crayons after doing just part of a coloring book's page." —*NEW YORK TIMES,* 24 May 1981

   f. "Adjective salad is delicious, with each element contributing its individual and unique flavor; but a puree of adjective soup tastes yecchy."
   —WILLIAM SAFIRE, *On Language*

4. Have students make a list of metaphors that use names of parts of the body. Such metaphors include

the *eye* of a hurricane	an *ear* of corn
the *brow* of a hill	the *foot* of a bed
the *nose* of an airplane	the *tongue* of a shoe
the *heart* of the matter	the *ribs* of a ship
bald cypress *knees*	the *hands* of a clock
the *face* of a cliff	the *elbow* of a river
a fine-*toothed* comb	a *cheeky* reply

Ask students to create similes for five of the italicized words. Or ask students to make a list of foods used metaphorically. Examples might include

cauliflower ears	a bread-and-butter note	
in a pickle	peach	
in a jam	peanut	
in a stew	shrimp	
a beefy wrangler	string bean	metaphors for people
a corny joke	honey	
salt-and-pepper hair	tomato	

5. Have students select words to complete the chart.

General	Specific	More Specific/Concrete
sport	_____	_____
_____	noun	_____
relationship	_____	_____
_____	_____	French fries
_____	perennials	_____

6. Have students compile a list of euphemisms associated with lying and then, as a class, write a paragraph using as many of them as possible.

ANSWERS TO EXERCISES

No answers are given for the dictionary exercises in this section, as answers will vary according to the dictionary used.

■ **Exercise 1** (p. 222–23)   **Correcting errors in diction and using exact words**

1. compost
2. childlike
3. flaunts
4. injustice
5. adapted
6. unfortunate
7. but OR ; however,
8. intimated
9. seasonal
10. affects

21

WORDINESS AND NEEDLESS REPETITION

Direct prose concentrates on the straightforward statement of ideas; nothing intervenes between ideas and precise diction. Economical prose wastes no words, thus keeping ideas vigorous; every word is spent profitably. The most ideas for the fewest words is the writer's goal; for just as one cup of tomato paste contains a tomato flavor more distilled than that in one cup of tomato juice, so direct, economical prose contains ideas more distilled than those in wordy prose.

In addition to diluting thoughts, wordy prose has other disadvantages. It shows the writer's inability to control the expression of ideas. It shows lack of respect for exact diction and for the audience, since wordy prose requires more time to read than economical prose. Compare, for example, the reading times of *After due consideration, the answer is affirmative* and *Yes.* In short, flabby diction is evidence of poor sentence tone.

Once beginning writers identify wordiness in their own prose, they are ready for systematic revisions. Simply cutting words often produces awkward or choppy sentences and restricts revision to one technique for intra-sentence problems. However, a method that applies omitting, rearranging, and combining within and between sentences gives writers an orderly series of options:

1. A compound predicate is reduced to one predicate.

   a. They *called* her *up* and *asked* her to advise them about selecting roses for a hedge.
   b. They *asked* her advice about selecting roses for a hedge.

2. A main clause becomes a subordinate clause.

   a. They asked her advice about selecting roses for a hedge.
   b. *When they asked her advice about selecting roses for a hedge,* she recommended floribundas for a hedge that would bloom continuously.

3. A subordinate clause becomes a phrase.

   a. When they asked her *what roses to select for a hedge,* she recommended floribundas for a hedge *that would bloom continuously.*
   b. When they asked her about *selecting roses for a hedge,* she recommended floribundas for a hedge *of continuous blooms.*

4. A phrase becomes a word.

   a. When they asked her about *selecting roses for a hedge,* she recommended floribundas *for a hedge of continuous blooms.*

b. When they asked her about *hedge roses,* she recommended *continuously blooming floribundas.*

5. Several words become one or are omitted entirely.

   a. When they asked *her* about *suggested* hedge roses, she *really strongly* recommended *a hedge of continuously everblooming* floribundas.
   b. When they asked about hedge roses, she recommended floribundas.

6. One sentence combines with another.

   a. When they asked about hedge roses, she recommended floribundas. She thought that for red roses they might like such varieties as "Europeana," "Vogue," and "Eutin."
   b. When they asked about hedge roses, she recommended three red floribundas: "Europeana," "Vogue," and "Eutin."
   c. "Europeana," "Vogue," and "Eutin" were the three varieties of red floribunda she recommended for their hedge.
   d. She recommended three red floribundas—"Europeana," "Vogue," and "Eutin"—for their hedge.

Students often have difficulty distinguishing between needless repetition (**21c**) and effective repetition for emphasis (**29e**) or coherence (**32b**). Three kinds of needless repetition are covered in **21c** and **21d**: unnecessarily repeating nouns or relative pronouns and using a word in two different senses. Judicious use of pronouns generally solves the first two problems; the substitution of a synonym solves the third. Students can often be helped to understand the difference between needless and effective repetition by seeing examples of each in context.

ACTIVITIES

1. Have students use direct, economical prose to revise these sentences:

   a. There are quite a few preparations at home to get ready for even today's modern picnic.
   b. The last and final step is the job of loading the necessities and things into the car. In this day and age the necessities often include Frisbees and volleyballs along with the food. This is done so that people will have something to do before the meal.
   c. After the windy gust, all the Styrofoam cups and paper plates on the picnic table were in an upset position. The major reason why they were was because Beth hadn't had time to fill the cups with lemonade drinks and lay the silverware on the plates.

2. Exercises do not replace having students reduce the wordiness in their own prose. To reduce the routine of the one-writer–one-essay class hour,

use a variety of approaches and have students work with sentences and paragraphs (reserve the revision of entire essays for homework assignments).

a. Have students number and write out or type (double space to allow room for revisions) sentences from one paragraph of a recent theme. Then ask students to revise each sentence two ways. Have students exchange papers and check the rewritten sentences for wordiness. Finally, have the writer use the revised and corrected sentences in a paragraph.

b. Bring to class a handout of wordy sentences from students' writing. Ask students to eliminate the wordiness and tell which of the six steps they used.

c. Have pairs of students revise a paragraph of each other's to eliminate wordiness.

d. Have two students work separately to revise the same paragraph; then, as a class, discuss which revisions are more effective. If pairing students would result in more than six or seven sets of paragraphs to discuss, consider having groups of three to six students work together to produce one revised paragraph.

3. Have students decide which passage contains needless repetition and revise it. Then ask them to explain why the repetition in the other passage is effective.

a. My happiest memory of fall is my memory of shuffling through the fall leaves that had fallen and that lay in big drifts across the sidewalks.

b. He laughs all the time: he laughs when he gets hurt; he laughs when he is praised; he laughs when he is idle; he laughs when he works.

ANSWERS TO EXERCISES

■ **Exercise 1** (p. 236)   **Revising to eliminate wordiness**

Answers will vary somewhat.

1. The exact date is not known.
2. During the last two innings, many senseless mistakes occurred.
3. Long lines of starving refugees were helped by Red Cross volunteers.
4. Perhaps the chief cause of obesity is lack of exercise.
5. The skyscrapers form a silhouette against the evening sky.

■ **Exercise 2** (pp. 236–37)   **Substituting one or two words for long phrases**

1. now OR today OR nowadays
2. can sing
3. believed

4. seriously
5. before
6. appeared
7. near
8. can OR may break
9. while
10. too expensive

■ **Exercise 3** (p. 237)   **Striking out unnecessary words**

1. It seems obvious.
2. Because Larry was there, the party was lively.
3. All these oil slicks, massive or not, do damage to the environment.
4. As for biased newscasts, I realize that reporters have to do some editing, though they may not use the finest judgment when underscoring some stories and downplaying others.

■ **Exercise 4** (pp. 237–38)   **Condensing sentences**

1. These are dangerous pitfalls.
2. This is an aggressive act.
3. It was a carefully planned garden.
4. It was a passionately delivered speech.
5. Her husband's dishes are not as good as her father's.
6. The students' ideas were different from the advertiser's.
7. Inevitably, corporations produce goods to make a profit.
8. Predictably, before an election legislators reduce taxation to win the approval of voters.
9. A pro-labor group wants two-month vacations.
10. One anti-"nuke" editorial stressed the need for state-controlled plants.

■ **Exercise 5** (p. 237)   **Reducing the number of words**

Answers will vary. The following are possibilities.

1. These invisible hazards cause many fatal accidents.
2. The United States was being invaded by foreign investors buying up farms.
3. Although my parents did not approve, I married Evelyn last June.
4. The fire chief recommended that wooden shingles not be used on homes.

■ **Exercise 6** (pp. 240–41)   **Eliminating wordiness and needless repetition**

1. The manager returned the application because of illegible handwriting.
2. It is difficult today to find a chemist who shows as much promise as Joseph Blake.
3. From time to time, a person needs to remember that anybody who is learning to walk has to put one foot before the other.
4. The yelling of fans in the stadium is so deafening that I stay home and watch the games on TV.

5. A distant hurricane or a seaquake can cause a tidal wave.
6. A comedy of intrigue (or of situation) relies on action rather than on characterization.
7. In my family, schoolwork came first, chores second, fun and games next, and discussions last.
8. Numerous products can be made from tobacco. Its nicotine is used in pesticides, and its sugar helps control blood pressure.

22

OMISSION OF NECESSARY WORDS

Whether omissions of necessary words result from the hurried, inaccurate recording of thoughts or the accurate recording of speech patterns, the effect is the same—a sentence that reads awkwardly and withholds a complete idea, thereby distracting the reader's attention until the omitted word is restored.

Three errors should receive special attention since they are made by students who usually proofread carefully for other omissions:

1. Prepositions omitted after verbs or other words—These omissions thwart the logical completion of the sentence, for example, *neither amused [by] nor interested in any explanation; overcome [by] and grateful for the comforting words; along [with] or in place of the salad.*

2. Elements in a comparison omitted—Comparisons are complete when the two subjects and the point of comparison are present. Thus, in the example in **22c**, *snow here* and *snow in Miami* are the subjects and *scarcity* is the point of comparison. But a sentence like *Wool is better for carpets* lacks the second subject, so that the point of comparison (*better*) is meaningless, yet such sentences occur frequently in commercial advertising as well as in students' writing.

3. Comma misused after *such*—When *such* is used as an intensifier, it is not separated from its clause by a comma (*He owns such a successful herbal tea company that he was a millionaire before he was thirty*). A comma is needed, however, when *such* occurs in parenthetical lists of examples (*Campers enjoy the outdoors in many ways, such as hiking, fishing, and bird-watching*).

ACTIVITIES

1. See Pence and Emery, *A Grammar of Present-Day English*, 2nd ed. (New York: Macmillan, 1963), for a list of prepositions used idiomatically. Ask students to use selected prepositions in sentences that illustrate differences in meaning (such as *adapted to, adapted from; need for, need of; compare to, compare with*).

2. Have students collect and rewrite examples of incomplete comparisons used in ads.

3. Ask students to write—but not to punctuate—sentences illustrating *such* used as an intensifier and as the head of a parenthetical list. Have students write the sentences on the chalkboard and ask others to provide the punctuation.

ANSWERS TO EXERCISES

■ **Exercise 1** (p. 244)   **Supplying needed words**

 1. Sheila *that* Richard
 2. kind *of* course
 3. *During the* winter
 4. *and* then OR dollar; then *she*
 5. was *that* my / pair *of* shoes
 6. ask *for* nor
 7. Fires *that* [OR *which*] had
 8. referred *to* was OR book *to* which
 9. exception *that* [OR *which*] proves
10. variety *of* spices

■ **Exercise 2** (p. 246)   **Supplying needed words**

 1. They *have* [OR *had*] been trying
 2. The consumers *had* better listen
 3. Ed's income is less than *that of* his wife.
    OR Ed's income is less than his wife*'s*.
 4. Bruce admires Cathy more than Aline *does*.
    OR Bruce admires Cathy more than *he does* Aline.
 5. Fiberglass roofs are better *than these.* [Answers will vary.]
 6. as any *other* place.
 7. I always have *liked*
 8. One argument was as bad *as*
 9. The ordinance never has *been*
10. more than the cranky young nurse *does*.
    OR more than *he does* the cranky young nurse.

■ **Exercise 3** (p. 246)   **Supplying needed words**

 1. I had *in* my senior year a strange type *of* virus.
 2. As far as Boston is *concerned,* I could see *that* the people
 3. The group is opposed *to*
 4. It *is* good to talk to a person *who* has a similar problem.
 5. as mild as *that in* Louisiana. OR as mild as *Louisiana's.*
 6. mysteries like *those involving* Sherlock Holmes.
 7. The lawyer had to prove *that*
 8. the hole *through* which the rabbit escaped.
 9. If Jack gets a job *for* which
10. people, and *they were* still coming.

23

SENTENCE UNITY

Sometimes students assume that because an essay is neatly typed and grammatically and mechanically correct it is also logically organized and soundly reasoned. That non sequitur then traps them into believing that a neat manuscript will conceal any faults in the writer's thinking.

Sentences that lack unity betray the writer's commitment to the central idea. While unrelated detail is probably more easily identified than excessive detail, students should understand that both undermine the effectiveness of the sentence—one by introducing extraneous material and the other by overwhelming the central idea in an attempt to provide adequate development for it. Apparently unrelated ideas are difficult for writers to identify since they understand the relationship and believe that what is obvious to them is obvious to the audience. A simple two-part question will help students avoid the problems: What is the relationship among ideas and how have I indicated it?

A mixed construction, which results from the use of parts of at least two possible statements, can be corrected by having students sort out the possibilities and choose the one they judge more effective. Here are two examples (from Exercise 3):

Because his feet are not the same size explains the difficulty he has finding shoes that fit.

1. Because his feet are not the same size, he has difficulty finding shoes that fit.
2. Having feet that are not the same size explains the difficulty he has finding shoes that fit.

Does anyone here know why George resigned or where did he find a better job?

1. Does anyone here know why George resigned or where he found a better job?
2. Why did George resign and where did he find a better job?

Students may wish to rewrite the sentences themselves to produce other alternatives.

An awkward definition (*Success is if you achieve your goal*) can be corrected by reviewing the parts of a formal definition (classification and differentiation or general category and distinguishing characteristics) and phrasing the definition so that the word being defined and the word identifying the classification are grammatically parallel (*Success is the achievement of a desired goal*).

When the logical connections between subject and verb break down, the result is faulty predication. Many, but not all, instances of faulty predication result from failure to recognize that the linking verb *be* serves as a kind of linguistic equals sign. Others are simply the result of confusion: In a sentence such as *Lions map the territory they claim for their own,* the predication is faulty because lions cannot map anything. Substituting the more accurate verb *mark* clears up the faulty predication.

ACTIVITIES

1. Ask students to discuss how the relationships between the ideas in the following sentences are not clear. Ask them to revise the sentences for unity.

   a. Although the visiting professor has different and refreshing views, I played badminton on September 20.
   b. The food in the cafeteria has been the subject of many jokes, and most college students do not look underfed.
   c. The ancient name for Paris, a city which has an annual rainfall of over 20 inches, was Lutetia.
   d. Brown hyenas are very shy animals and have an interesting social organization.

2. Ask students to discuss how to eliminate excessive detail from the following sentences:

   a. During eight o'clock classes last Thursday in room 331 of MacIntyre Hall which is where most of the history classes are held, the debate team held a practice debate to which all of the students enrolled in speech classes were invited.
   b. When I was about ten, tall for my age, and living in a house built during the colonial period, little of which remains today, I often walked several miles to play with neighbor children.
   c. As the classic old boat made of wood rather than the more modern fiberglass turned into the wind which was blowing about eight or ten miles an hour, the new sails were hoisted by the crew who were all medical students at the university but who welcomed the chance to get away from their heavy study schedules for an afternoon and perhaps an evening.

3. Have students identify mixed metaphors, mixed constructions, or faulty predication in the following sentences before having them revise the sentences. This exercise works well as a group activity.

   a. Although Sarah was burning the candle at both ends, she realized the need to keep her nose to the grindstone.
   b. Does the chairman of the board ride in a limousine or carry his briefcase to the office?
   c. The use of biomechanical research developed options to organ transplants.

ANSWERS TO EXERCISES

■ **Exercise 1** (p. 249)   **Rewriting to relate ideas**

1. There are so many types of bores at social gatherings that I prefer quiet evenings at home.
2. A telephone lineman who works during heavy storms can prove a hero. Of course, cowards can be found in any walk of life.
3. Jones was advised to hire a tutor in French immediately. Long hours of work at the florist shop kept his grades low.
4. Professor Stetson, who likes to draw parallels between modern men and literary characters, pointed out that Macbeth was not the only man to succumb to ambition.
5. In the summer birds get food by eating worms and insects that are pests to farmers. As insects become scarce in the fall, the birds migrate to warmer countries where insects are plentiful.

■ **Exercise 2** (p. 250)   **Eliminating excessive detail**

1. The fan that Joan bought for her brother arrived today. He frets about any temperature that exceeds seventy.
2. Flames from the gas heater licked at the chintz curtains.
3. After finishing breakfast, Sigrid called the tree surgeon.
4. At last I returned the library book that I had used for my Tuesday report.
5. A course in business methods helps undergraduates to get jobs and tests their fitness for business.

■ **Exercise 3** (p. 250)   **Eliminating mixed or awkward constructions**

1. Another famous story from American history is the one about Christopher Columbus.
2. One example of a rip-off would be the addition of a butcher's heavy thumb to the weight of the steak.
3. To have good manners is to avoid saying or doing something tactless.
4. Like a bat guided by radar, Mark was always careful in business dealings.
5. Could anyone be certain why George resigned or where he found a better job?
6. For Don, money does grow on trees, and he frequently shakes the limbs.
7. He has difficulty finding shoes that fit because his feet are not the same size.
8. I felt as insignificant as a grain of sand in the desert.
9. When children need glasses they may make mistakes in reading and writing.
10. The National Weather Service predicted subnormal temperatures in late March.

24

SUBORDINATION

Subordination and coordination both involve combining two or more simple sentences to create a new sentence in which the grammatical relationship(s) between the ideas is clearly defined. When one idea is subordinated to another, it is said to be of lesser grammatical rank. That is, it operates on the secondary level of the sentence (as do adjectives and other modifiers). However, although a subordinate clause is said to be of lesser grammatical rank, it is not necessarily of lesser rhetorical importance. Compare:

1. Sarah, who lived in Des Moines for six years, has just received her commercial pilot's license. [The subordinate element contains information unrelated to and of lesser importance than the main clause.]
2. As soon as Sarah flew to Seattle, Beth and I drove to Portland. [The subordinate clause establishes the time relationship and is just as important as the main clause.]
3. Although your request for a five-thousand-dollar raise has been denied, you will receive two more paid holidays. [The negative information in the subordinate clause is rhetorically more important than the positive information in the main clause.]

For a useful discussion of subordination as a principle, see Margaret Bryant, *A Functional English Grammar* (Boston: Heath, 1945) 176–79.

When two simple sentences are coordinated, they are said to be of equal grammatical rank, and, ideally, they are of equal rhetorical importance. Occasionally, however, they may not be equally important rhetorically. Compare:

1. Tom sent Judy's gift to Grand Isle and Judy sent Tom's gift to Birmingham. [The two clauses contain information of equal grammatical and rhetorical importance.]
2. Tom cancelled his trip to Grand Isle, for Judy had already left for Europe. [Although both clauses are of equal grammatical importance, the first clause might well be of greater rhetorical importance than the second.]

Students often do not understand that coordination normally establishes an equal relationship between clauses. Rather, they see coordination as a convenient way to link ideas without developing them. Believing that *and* is a transition that guarantees paragraph unity, beginning writers often link everything with *and,* creating prose that offers no relief for the reader. A useful stylistic point to emphasize to students is that professional writers use a large percentage of complex sentences and that compound sentences are relatively rare.

ACTIVITIES

1. Ask students to write a main clause containing a subject, a verb, and a direct object. Have students exchange papers and add one subordinate clause. Repeat, again asking for a subordinate clause. Repeat, asking for one set of coordinate elements. Have students read and discuss the resulting sentences.

2. Ask students to write down three goals they want to achieve before the end of the semester. Have them rank the goals from most important to least important and then write a sentence using subordination to reflect the ranking. Ask them to follow the same procedure for three goals to be met within a year, three before they graduate, and three within five years after graduation.

3. Ask students to combine the following sentences in as many ways as possible and to identify which idea is stressed in each. Have them begin with coordination and then move to subordination.

   a. 1. I was walking through the park.
      2. An elderly lady was walking through the park.
      3. A thief stole the elderly lady's purse.

   b. 1. Marlene is a dentist.
      2. Her hobby is breeding tropical fish.
      3. Her husband is a film editor.
      4. His hobby is baking bread.

   c. 1. Eloise and Donald were waiting for a table.
      2. Two women dressed in evening gowns were seated at a table beside the window.
      3. A waiter spilled tangerine sherbet on one woman.

4. Too many elements in a sentence impede the main idea. Have students suggest revisions for these sentences:

   a. The family who bought that custom-designed ranch house that Avery Realty had on the market for eight months when sales were especially slow decided to ask that the previous owners return the water softener which was to remain in the house.

   b. Wearing the furry hat that his grandchildren who lived in Bismarck had given him when they learned that the only one he had was a green felt one that belonged to his brother who knew how cold North Dakota winters were, Carl walked to the diner where the owner cooked breakfast and said that a hungry man could eat three eggs as easily as two, so three eggs were what a customer would always get.

ANSWERS TO EXERCISES

The following revisions are suggestions. Many other revisions for subordination are possible.

■ **Exercise 1** (p. 258)   **Using subordination to combine short sentences**

[1,2]Now that I have just read "The Idea of a University," I am especially interested in Newman's views regarding knowledge. [3,4,5]Newman says that knowledge is a treasure in itself, that it is its own reward, not just a means to an end. [6,7,8]Before reading this essay, I had looked upon knowledge only in terms of practical results—such as financial security. [9,10]Now I accept Newman's definition of knowledge, which is worth pursuing for its own sake.

■ **Exercise 2** (p. 259)   **Using subordination to improve sentence unity**

1. After she had selected a lancet and sterilized it, she gave the patient a local anesthetic and lanced the infected flesh.
2. I did not hear the telephone ring yesterday because I was taking a shower, but I got the message in time to go to the party.
3. Although an oncoming bus crowded a truckload of laborers off the road when the two ambulances tore by, nobody got hurt.
4. Because Jean Henri Dunant, a citizen of Switzerland, felt sorry for Austrian soldiers wounded in the Napoleonic Wars, he started an organization, which was later named the Red Cross.
5. Stressing career education, the administrators not only required back-to-basics courses but also kept students informed about job opportunities.

■ **Exercise 3** (p. 260)   **Simple, compound, and complex sentences**

Answers will vary.

1. a. The men were sentenced to six years in prison for smuggling marijuana into Spain.
   b. The men smuggled marijuana into Spain, so they were sentenced to six years in prison.
   c. The men who smuggled marijuana into Spain were sentenced to six years in prison.
2. a. After condemning the property, the council ordered the owner's eviction.
   b. The council first condemned the property; then, it ordered the owner's eviction.
   c. After the council condemned the property, it ordered the owner's eviction.

3. a. Having applied for a patent on his invention, Uncle Oliver learned of three hundred such devices already on the market.
    b. Uncle Oliver applied for a patent on his invention, but he learned of three hundred such devices already on the market.
    c. When Uncle Oliver applied for a patent on his invention, he learned of three hundred such devices already on the market.
4. a. Delaying every tourist, the border guards carefully examined passports and luggage.
    b. The border guards delayed every tourist, for they carefully examined passports and luggage.
    c. The border guards delayed every tourist while they carefully examined passports and luggage.

25

MISPLACED PARTS, DANGLING MODIFIERS

It is not enough to collect words, capitalize the first one, place a period after the last one, and call the result a sentence. While students would readily agree that *Boldly dog cat the hissed at* is ungrammatical, they have more difficulty with dangling constructions because the words follow English syntax. The misplaced or dangling parts and the related part(s) are themselves grammatical. The logical bridge (whether a word or word order), however, is not. But because students are satisfied with the meaning they derive (in a sentence like *It only costs fifty dollars*) or because they supply the bridge, perhaps without realizing they are doing so (in a sentence like *Walking through the house, clutter greeted her everywhere,* which produces two ideas: *She was walking through the house* and *Clutter greeted her everywhere*), they do not recognize the flaw.

Since a writer cannot depend on readers either to be satisfied or to supply the logical connection, the writer must create coherent sentences. Not doing so risks the reader's laughter as the word order calls up comical, outlandish, or outrageous images that detract from the main idea. Students find the sentences in dangling-modifier exercises laughable; you might point out that those dangling modifiers in students' papers are no less laughable.

ACTIVITIES

1. Ask students to discuss the differences in meaning:
   a. 1. Only Jamie said that the novel was inspiring.
      2. Jamie only said that the novel was inspiring.
      3. Jamie said only that the novel was inspiring.
      4. Jamie said that only the novel was inspiring.
      5. Jamie said that the only novel was inspiring.
      6. Jamie said that the novel was only inspiring.

   b. 1. Almost everyone was in tears.
      2. Everyone was almost in tears.

   c. 1. Merely sweeping the floor once a week is satisfactory.
      2. Sweeping merely the floor once a week is satisfactory.
      3. Sweeping the floor merely once a week is satisfactory.
      4. Sweeping the floor once a week is merely satisfactory.

2. Ask students to revise each sentence, eliminating "squinting" modifiers and split infinitives.

    a. Chewing gum slowly calms his nerves.

    b. To entirely remove gum from a shag rug requires patiently scraping gum that has been rubbed with an ice cube repeatedly.

    c. Scraping often takes more patience than I have.

    d. Let's remember to have always guaranteed gum remover just in case we have this problem again.

3. Have students identify the absolute phrases, sentence modifiers, and dangling modifiers in these sentences.

    a. Entering the discussion of favorite authors, Jane Austen and Kurt Vonnegut were mentioned first. [DM]

    b. The conversation having been prompted by Rachel's enthusiasm for Flannery O'Connor's writing, we began to compile a list of favorite female authors. [AP]

    c. Speaking of contemporary fiction, who has read Gail Godwin's novels? [SM]

    d. Kevin suggested the stories of Elizabeth Bowen saying that Caroline Gordon's stories were also some of his favorites. [DM]

    e. Considering the number of books published every year, I would like to read two or three a week. [SM]

    f. Feeling fortunate to read two or three a month, the number of must-read books grows faster than I can keep up with. [DM]

    g. Fiction being put aside for now, my next project is to read every book on the nonfiction best-seller list. [AP]

4. Ask students to rewrite the sentences from one paragraph of a recent theme by using absolute phrases, sentence modifiers, and elliptical adverbial clauses.

ANSWERS TO EXERCISES

■ **Exercise 1** (p. 263)   **Placing single-word modifiers correctly**

1. killed *only* one person
2. cost *nearly* fifty dollars
3. ate *almost* all the turkey
4. show *hardly* any interest

■ **Exercise 2** (p. 263)   **Bringing related parts together**

1. Newspapers in every part of the country
2. date muffins with pecans in them
3. sundaes in paper cups
4. On Monday the professor made it clear

- **Exercise 3** (p. 264)   **Eliminating squinting modifiers or needless separation of related parts**

1. An official warned the hunter not to carry a loaded rifle in the car.
2. Selby said he would go in the evening. OR In the evening Selby said he would go.
3. Because he was winning, Marvin wanted to finish the game.
4. Harriet promised to stop at the library on her way home.
5. The car advertised in last night's paper is only two years old and is in excellent condition.

- **Exercise 4** (pp. 266–67)   **Eliminating dangling modifiers**

Answers may vary somewhat.

1. While I was wondering about this phenomenon, the sun sank from view.
2. We ended the meeting by standing and repeating the pledge.
3. Once made, the decision must be promptly executed.
4. Prepare to make an incision in the abdomen as soon as the patient is completely anesthetized.
5. After we had sat there awhile, it began to snow, and we went indoors.
6. CORRECT
7. After the witness had taken his seat, we began to question him.
8. Just as we were ready to pitch camp, the windstorm hit.
9. CORRECT
10. Because their house had burned to the ground, the Welches had to build a new one.

- **Exercise 5** (p. 267)   **Using introductory parenthetical elements to combine sentences**

Answers may vary somewhat.

1. Having a broken arm and nose, the statue is, I think, an interesting antique.
2. When worried about the world situation, James sometimes thought it would be a good idea to join the Peace Corps.
3. After reading the first three questions, I realized that the test covered materials that I had not studied.
4. Only twelve years old, Larry had inventive abilities that his teachers noticed.
5. Turning on the flashers and lifting the hood, I thought that a passing motorist might see my predicament, slow down, and offer me a ride.

26
PARALLELISM

A special kind of coordination, parallelism strengthens writing in several ways. Because it relies on repetition of grammatical structures, it is a particularly effective way to present complementary or contrasting ideas. When several complementary ideas are to be expressed, their similarity is heightened and coherence is improved if they are expressed in constructions that correspond to each other. (Some parallel constructions occur so frequently that they may not be recognized as such—compound subjects and objects, coordinate adjectives. Others call attention to themselves through the deliberate repetition of lengthy structures or the use of signal words such as *not only* and *but also*.) Arranging parallel items in climactic order emphasizes the items themselves as well as their degrees of importance. Finally, parallelism is perhaps the most common means of achieving balance and rhythmic flow in prose. Of course, neglecting other techniques for achieving emphasis or coherence in favor of parallelism can lead to monotony.

ACTIVITIES

1. Ask students to write down a series of parallel sentences beginning with *I know that.* Although students begin with the obvious (*I know that today is Tuesday. I know that tomorrow is Wednesday*), as a rule they move on to more reflective thoughts. In any event, they are practicing parallel forms in addition to characterizing themselves by the pieces of information they choose to include. Such constructions as *To _____ is to _____* or *I remember when _____* may also be used.

2. Ask students to write a six-sentence paragraph using at least one set of parallel elements in every sentence. Then have students revise the paragraph, saving only the most effective parallel constructions.

3. Ask students to write one sentence containing coordinate nouns, verbs, infinitive phrases, participial phrases, and dependent clauses (*Wearing cowboy gear and swaggering through the crowd to advertise the rodeo and to promote Laramie Days, the father and son laughed and whooped as they greeted visitors and even while they sold tickets.*). Have students label each coordinate pair or revise the sentence if any element is missing.

ANSWERS TO EXERCISES

■ **Exercise 1** (p. 270)   **Underlining parallel structures**

1. bees, birds, or bats.
2. bought by the yard and worn by the foot.
3. To say that some truths are simple . . . to say they are unimportant.
4. Reading through *The Origin* . . . eating Cracker Jacks and finding an IOU note.
5. mountains taller than Everest, valleys deeper than the Dead Sea rift, and highlands bigger than Australia
6. who do not need flowers, who cannot be surprised by joy
7. Booms attract an oversupply; busts generate an undersupply.
8. Think before you speak. Read before you think.

■ **Exercise 2** (p. 271)   **Inserting words needed for parallel structure**

1. *a* day OR *for a* day
2. *to* succeed
3. *that* I had reasons
4. *by* worrying
5. *an* elephant OR *of an* elephant

■ **Exercise 3** (p. 272)   **Using parallel structures for parallel ideas**

1. to play tennis and *to watch* basketball
2. both heredity and *environment*
3. whether the trip would be delayed or *whether I would be ready to start on Friday*
4. quiet and *serious*
5. the workers and *the dependents*

27
SHIFTS

Coherent prose—writing that is consistent, orderly, and logical—usually includes shifts made necessary by the content: the mood of verbs changes from indicative to subjunctive as the writer distinguishes a fact from a condition contrary to fact; direct discourse alternates with indirect discourse to indicate shifts from speech to thought. Such shifts are needed because they help develop the writer's message.

Some shifts, however, produce inconsistencies that destroy coherence by sending out conflicting information about the relationship of ideas. In the first pair of sentences in **27a**, for example, the shift of tenses from *argued* to *discusses* conflicts with words showing that the activities are simultaneous (*during, while*). In the second example the shift from subjunctive to indicative not only signals an illogical condition but also weakens the parallel structure. Such shifts as these obscure the meaning and interfere with coherence.

ACTIVITIES

1. Ask students to identify the needless shifts in the following sentences:

   a. If I was poor and you were rich, would we still be friends?
   b. David has been nominated to fill the vacancy, and almost everyone agrees he would be a conscientious chairman.
   c. One should practice daily if you want to be a concert violinist.
   d. Those who have done our best should never be apologetic.

2. Have students write a paragraph alternating the direct discourse of two speakers and the indirect discourse of a third person.

3. Bring to class copies of one or two student paragraphs and ask students to correct any needless shifts and to justify any needed ones. Or ask students to justify the shifts they find in a professionally written essay.

ANSWERS TO EXERCISES

■ **Exercise 1** (pp. 275–76)   **Correcting needless shifts**

Answers may vary somewhat.

1. asked
2. and that the money be spent

3. he baked it for fifteen minutes
4. All bystanders were
5. that *one* should bathe

■ **Exercise 2** (p. 277)   **Correcting needless shifts**

1. grabbed . . . snatched
2. All enjoy a vacation
3. CORRECT
4. and whether he had said when he would return.
5. All cooks have
6. there was
7. CORRECT but *him* OR *her* OR *him/her* is often preferred
8. You will need it. OR It will be needed.
9. fortress; inside, the
10. and whether I would take the makeup quiz on Tuesday.

■ **Exercise 3** (p. 277)   **Eliminating needless shifts**

Answers will vary. The following are possibilities.

[1]He is a shrewd businessman, or so it has always seemed to me. [2]He has innocent-looking eyes, which are in a baby face, and swaggers when he walks. [3]When questioned about his recent windfall, he says, "I'm lucky enough to have the right contacts." [4]Not one name does he mention; moreover, he is reluctant to discuss his business transactions. [5]These comments should be taken for what they are worth. They may help one who deals with this shrewd businessman.

28

REFERENCE OF PRONOUNS

The clarity of pronoun-antecedent references depends not only on agreement in person and number but also on the proximity of a specific, expressed antecedent for the pronoun. Thus, broad reference or intervening words may create ambiguity or obscurity that interferes with the reader's understanding of ideas. Although experienced writers may occasionally use broad reference, it rarely increases clarity and precision, so students would profit more by concentrating on the constructions that do. To ensure clarity, inexperienced writers may be advised to make each of their pronouns refer to a specific word.

Every writer, experienced or inexperienced, must recognize the different meanings of *it* in order to avoid confusing the reader. To change meanings when repeating a word within a sentence violates the reader's one-word–one-meaning expectation. Thus, these various meanings of *it* should not be placed near each other:

1. *it* as pronoun (*I read the book as soon as I bought it.*)
2. *it* as an expletive (*It is not surprising that he won a scholarship. It is impossible for them to sing on key.*)
3. *it* as an indefinite in expression of time or weather (*It is raining. It is noon.*)
4. *it* as an indefinite in the *it* + noun + *who* or *that* construction (*It is Larry who suggested a scholarship to honor Professor Williams.*)
5. *it* as a word (*One of the original forms of it was hit.*)

ACTIVITIES

1. Ask students to revise each sentence in three ways: by repeating the antecedent, by using a synonym, and by recasting the sentence.

   a. When four-year-old Cory and two-year-old Brad play together, he always knocks down the blocks.
   b. Our daughter prefers looking through her microscope to cleaning her room. This takes up at least two hours every Saturday morning.
   c. As Greg and his uncle shook hands, he thanked him for the helmet and jersey.

2. Ask students to eliminate the broad reference in each of the following:

   a. They accepted our challenge to play softball once a week. This means we'll have to practice seriously if we expect to win.
   b. Her research paper was written, her finals had been canceled, and her aunt had sent her one hundred dollars. That was not the case for her roommate.

3. Have students revise each sentence to eliminate ambiguous, remote, or obscure references.

   a. If you say it, then it's true that he practices the piano ten hours a day.
   b. It's seven-thirty and it's still raining, but it will pass soon.
   c. Buy them a damask tablecloth or sew them some calico napkins and placemats. It won't matter because they are both nice.
   d. It's a fact that it hasn't been the same since Mary left.
   e. Because Chris had budgeted wisely, it meant he could buy a new tape deck. Which he had been looking forward to for more than a year.

4. Select two or three letters from an advice column and have students identify the antecedent for each pronoun. Have students use pronouns in writing an answer to one letter not discussed in class.

ANSWERS TO EXERCISES

■ **Exercise 1** (p. 280)   **Eliminating ambiguous, remote, or obscure reference**

Answers may vary. The following are possibilities.

1. The tiff between the two families did not end until the Kemps invited the Dixons over for a swim in their new pool.
2. buttons and knobs that are clearly labeled seldom cause confusion
3. In her letter, Jane did not mention the robbery.
4. peaceful. It is well stocked with fish. Near the shore
5. As Meg was coming down the ramp, she waved to Mrs. James.

■ **Exercise 2** (pp. 282–83)   **Correcting faulty reference of pronouns**

Answers may vary. The following are possibilities.

1. but chow mein is their favorite food.
2. water leaked all over the kitchen floor.
3. assistants can manage these machines easily and quickly.
4. The article states that
5. CORRECT
6. My failure even to buy a season ticket was very disloyal to my school.
7. "I have to read *Pride and Prejudice*," Mary told Ann.
8. might cover the roads and make them useless.
9. Extra fees that seemed unreasonably high surprised many freshmen.
10. Frank packs only wash-and-wear clothes in his suitcase.

29
EMPHASIS

Writers choose a number of ways to achieve proper emphasis for their ideas. They may deliberately structure a sentence so that the key words appear either at the beginning or the end—the most important positions in a sentence, or they may use a periodic sentence, reserving the main idea for the end of the sentence and leading up to it with less important details. Similarly, writers arrange ideas in an order of climax to emphasize what they consider to be most important. These three techniques are similar in that they rely on placement to create the emphasis. But writers also achieve emphasis through diction—by choosing active verbs that are forceful and vigorous or by selecting important words for repetition. Finally, writers construct balanced sentences of varied lengths to signal to readers that certain ideas are important.

Once students have decided which ideas are most important and why, they are ready to try out these techniques—one at a time or in combination—until they find the most effective one for each idea. Experimenting with the options, students eventually come to rely on three or four with which they feel most comfortable; they should be encouraged to use other techniques occasionally, too. Finally, students should look at each sentence in the context of the whole paragraph; if any technique is ineffective or overused, revision is called for.

ACTIVITIES

1. Have students select four sentences from a paragraph of their favorite theme. Ask students to rewrite the sentences using each of the eight techniques in Section **29** for each of the sentences and to devise some simple tabular arrangement that will allow them to compare the resulting sentences. Students will see that they may have already used some techniques and that not all methods suit every sentence.

   For each of the original sentences, have students select the revision they find most effective. Ask the students which methods they are most comfortable with. Have them put their favorite revised sentences into a paragraph and make any changes necessary for ease of reading.

2. Have students use another paragraph which they enjoyed writing or which they think is particularly effective. Ask them to rewrite the paragraph using any three of the eight emphasis techniques. Once they finish, ask them to label each use. Then have them rewrite the paragraph using three of the remaining five methods. Ask them which paragraph they prefer. The goal here is not to achieve flawless arrangements but to explore the possible

combinations; the discovery of combinations that do not work well together is just as valuable as the discovery of those that do.

3. Have groups of students write a paragraph consisting of one topic sentence, one or two sentences of support, one or two sentences of examples, and a concluding sentence. All sentences should be in subject-verb-object order, in active voice, in loose rather than periodic structure, and of approximately equal length. Ask groups of students to exchange and rewrite paragraphs.

4. Have students analyze one body paragraph from a recent theme by answering these questions:

   a. How many sentences does the paragraph contain?
   b. How many words does each sentence contain? What is the average number of words per sentence?
   c. In which sentences are important words at the beginning or end?
   d. Which sentences are loose?
   e. Which sentences use the order of climax?
   f. Which sentences use active voice?
   g. What are the one or two most important words? How often is each word repeated?
   h. Not counting dangling modifiers, how many times are words emphasized by being out of usual order? Which sentences are inverted? How many of the inverted sentences are questions?
   i. Which sentences are balanced?

   After students answer these questions, ask them to list conclusions drawn from the analysis. Have them write a paragraph describing their methods of emphasis and suggesting one way to improve their arrangement of ideas.

5. Ask students to analyze one paragraph from a published essay.

ANSWERS TO EXERCISES

■ **Exercise 1** (p. 285)   **Revising for emphasis**

Answers will vary. The following are possibilities.

1. Music has the power to hypnotize.
2. Only one person could have written all these articles because of their same political slant.
3. One stunt woman earns five thousand dollars for two hours of work.
4. Never before had it entered her mind to resent her husband's complacent ignorance or to ignore his unreasonable demands.

■ **Exercise 2** (pp. 286–87) **Converting loose sentences into periodic, periodic into loose**

Answers may vary somewhat. The following are possibilities.

1. Despite everything, Italy remains cheerful.
2. Old habits and reflexes persist, even where people want better relations.
3. The Milky Way Galaxy, one of billions of other galaxies strewn through the vastness of space, is entirely unremarkable.
4. Nervously backing away from the arguments she should have had with my father, turning aside from the talks she should have had with me, she was then (as always, as she had been all her life) sweet and apologetic.
5. "I just oppose it if I don't know anything about something, or if I don't understand it," Mays told me, almost with pride.

■ **Exercise 3** (pp. 287–88) **Arranging ideas in order of climax**

Answers may vary somewhat. The following are possibilities.

1. industry, efficiency, and wisdom
2. sun-drenched orchards, golden-flecked birds, and diamond-eyed children
3. his pet dog was tired of the leash, his taxes were going up, and his health was failing
4. The commission is faced with a deficit. Something must be done at once. Unless we act now, the city will be bankrupt in five years.
5. autographed books for teenagers, wrote letters to senior citizens, attended a community festival, and promised prosperity to all.

■ **Exercise 4** (p. 289) **Substituting active for passive voice; using forceful verbs**

1. Tourists often throw pennies into the fountain.
2. My brother manipulates other people.
3. Every Saturday, easily influenced children watch TV.
4. Bad pizza tastes like cardboard.
5. The citizens greatly fear that the judge will sentence the defendant too harshly.

■ **Exercise 5** (pp. 289–90) **Using repetition instead of synonyms**

1. Sometimes we lie . . . ; sometimes we lie
2. . . . he gripes about the weather, gripes about heavy traffic, gripes about high prices, and gripes about his meals.

■ **Exercise 9** (pp. 291–92) **Revising for emphasis**

Answers will vary. The following are possibilities.

1. Replacing human organs with animal organs, even if it extends a person's life, should stop.
2. Jokes referring to minorities or to religion offend many people.
3. All around us were fields of wild flowers.

4. Fools talk about each other; wise people talk about ideas.
5. When the fleeing youth tripped over the patrolman's foot, the gun fired.
6. At the close of a hot day, the storm broke in all its fury.
7. Milburn caught a fast pass and gained thirty yards before the referee blew the whistle.
8. Two years ago, late in the fall, in a shop on Tremont Street, I asked her to marry me.
9. Although their art was crude, some of the people showed a great deal of originality.
10. By the simple device of choosing the least likely suspect whose alibi is airtight, I can identify the guilty person in every Agatha Christie novel.

30
VARIETY

Emphasis is the arrangement of ideas in a sentence to highlight their relative importance. Variety is the arrangement of sentences to create changes in both structure and length that keep the reader's attention on the flow of ideas. Since most students begin their sentences with the subject and give little or no thought to the length of their sentences, sentence beginnings and varying length are the first topics to discuss.

Sentence lengths do not vary according to some arbitrary rule, such as twenty words, eight words, twelve words, two longs, a short, and a long. Lengths do vary according to the kinds of information presented. Because it involves qualifications of and relationships among ideas, adequate development—explanations, illustrations, and other supporting material—tends to require sentences that are longer than topic sentences or transitions. But not all supporting sentences are long—an abrupt change in length may be used for emphasis. And not all topic sentences are short—they may include a transition in addition to the several ideas directing the paragraph. Variation for its own sake is ineffective; the goal is variation that attends to the needs of both the ideas and the audience.

In addition to the suggestions in **30b** for varying sentence beginnings, you might use these patterns:

1. an infinitive or infinitive phrase (*To cut the logs into firewood, he used a chain saw.*)
2. an introductory series (*The porcelain vase, the hand-painted platter, and the domed butter dish—these the movers packed in a special carton.*)
3. a noun clause as either subject or direct object (*That they kept their promise pleases me.*)

ACTIVITIES

1. Have students write a paragraph of five or six sentences, each sentence beginning with the subject and consisting of twelve to fifteen words. Ask students to rewrite the paragraph, varying both sentence lengths and beginnings. Then have students exchange papers and revise the original paragraph. Ask them to discuss the merits of each revised paragraph. (If class size prevents a whole-group discussion of all the paragraphs, divide students into groups of three and proceed as above.)

2. Have students analyze one paragraph from the first theme of the semester

and one from the most recent theme by answering these questions for each:

a. How many words does each sentence contain? What is the longest sentence? Why? (complexity of ideas, wordiness, and so on) What is the shortest sentence? Why? Where does it occur? (beginning, middle, end)

b. Which sentences are declarative? interrogative? imperative? exclamatory?

c. Which sentences begin with the subject? a sentence connective? an adverb? an adverb clause? a prepositional phrase? a participial phrase? an infinitive? an infinitive phrase? an appositive? an absolute? a series? a noun clause?

d. Which sentences are simple? compound? complex? compound-complex?

e. In which sentences do words intervene between the subject and verb?

Asking students *which* sentences, instead of merely how many, requires them to look closely at patterns and to discover whether the variety, if any, is confined to one section of the paragraph or is evenly distributed throughout. Have students describe their findings by writing a one-paragraph summary for each paragraph analyzed.

3. Have students choose three ways of varying sentence structure and include them in the revision of one paragraph from a recent theme. Then have students revise the original paragraph again by using three different methods.

4. Ask students to prepare to discuss Exercises 3 and 7 (or paragraphs they have collected) by answering the questions used to analyze their own prose.

ANSWERS TO EXERCISES

■ **Exercise 2** (pp. 295–96)   **Combining sentences to relate ideas**

Answers will vary. The following are possibilities.

1. With thirty seconds of play left, Harrison intercepted the pass, raced downfield, and dropped the ball at the five-yard line.

2. Her speech had an interesting thesis: salespersons should not only solve the existing problems of their customers but should also point out new problems in order to solve them.

3. Bennett's Comet, which appeared in 1969 and disappeared in 1970, will not be visible again for thousands of years.

4. Instead of buying a second car, Ellen Dolan bought a Piper, a small airplane, which flies at almost a hundred miles an hour.

5. In his book *Kinship with All Life,* J. Allen Boone describes his ability to

communicate with animals; he converses mentally with a dog; he orders ants to leave his home, and they obey; he even tames an ordinary house-fly.

■ **Exercise 4** (p. 298)   **Recasting sentences to vary the beginnings**

Answers will vary. The following are possibilities.

1. a. Asking some very tricky questions about world affairs, reporters inter-viewed the newly appointed Secretary.
   b. During the interview, reporters asked the newly appointed Secretary some very tricky questions about world affairs.
2. a. Today, many people are concerned about the quality of life but not about a reverence for life.
   b. Although concerned about the quality of life, many people today are not concerned about a reverence for life.
3. a. Most of all, Jesse enjoyed the course in science fiction literature.
   b. The course in science fiction literature Jesse enjoyed most of all.
4. a. Traveling at great speed, the green fireballs fascinated sky watchers throughout the Southwest.
   b. Sky watchers throughout the Southwest were fascinated by green fire-balls traveling at great speed.

■ **Exercise 5** (p. 300)   **Revising loose, stringy compound sentences**

Answers will vary. The following are possibilities.

1. Even though the small car hugs the road and is easy to drive in traffic, it is not comfortable.
2. Growing tired of city smog and noise pollution, the Johnsons moved to the country, where they had no fire department or police protection.
3. After first trading their products and then using money and bank checks, Americans now use the all-inclusive plastic credit card.
4. Mentioning such things as marriage and two-car garages, Harvey kept criticizing middle-class values, but he did not define upper-class or lower-class values.

■ **Exercise 6** (p. 301)   **Varying subject-verb sequence**

Answers will vary. The following are possibilities.

1. Roger, like his mother, is an excellent conversationalist.
2. Rhode Island, east of Connecticut, has a forty-mile coastline.
3. My grandparents, valuing strong family ties, encouraged us young ones "to always keep in touch."
4. Margaret, racing back to the library to avoid getting wet, fell broadside into a big puddle of water.
5. Wizzard Wells, a popular resort once, is a ghost town now.

31

LOGICAL THINKING

Because students frequently feel intimidated by the study of logic, a low-keyed, matter-of-fact approach does much to allay their fears. Instructors might begin by expanding on the approach used in Section **31** to begin both inductive and deductive reasoning, leading students to recognize how much logic they already use naturally and easily. Drawing upon decisions students are commonly faced with helps them to master the principles of induction and deduction before they examine the logic of their own writing. Using selection of a major, for instance, the instructor might ask students to draw up a list of the pros and cons of choosing a particular major—engineering and pre-med elicit good responses. After the reasons are listed, have students discuss the logic behind each reason.

When students have examined their own decision-making, they are better able to examine the decisions of others to support or oppose popular issues; here it is important not that students agree with the decisions but that they analyze the logic of the argument. Students should examine their position on one popular issue (sufficiently narrowed and clearly defined) by, as suggested above, listing their reasons for supporting or opposing the issue and then discussing the logic of the reasons they have listed. Once they are sure that the reasons are logically sound, they may proceed to argue them in an essay.

When students feel relatively comfortable with induction and deduction, instructors should move on to a discussion of fallacies. Section **31** discusses a number of the fallacies most common in student writing. Instructors may wish to add others—drawn from experience as well as from logic textbooks available in almost any college library.

Once alerted to the value of logic in writing, students often enjoy dissecting the logical fabric of short passages and even of short essays. Such activities strengthen students' understanding of persuasive discourse and improve their ability to write it.

Note: Although the study of logic for its own sake can be fascinating for both students and instructor, it is usually a good idea to avoid the finer points of formal logic—for example, those concerning Venn diagrams and warrants—unless a class is especially receptive.

ACTIVITIES

1. Ask students to list and discuss the pros and cons of renting an apartment rather than a dorm room; attending summer school rather than working full time during the summer; attending their present school rather than a close rival; going to college immediately after high school graduation rather than

waiting a year or so. Ask them to identify any logical fallacies in the reasons.

2. Have students use logical fallacies to write commercials for products of their choice.

3. Have students contrast the assumptions of arguments given by opposing sides on some campus issue.

4. Have students discuss the use of induction and deduction in the following passage:

> Proponents of economic specialization would of course attack the idea that import replacing is economically constructive. Specialization, they would argue, represents the division of labor on a regional or an international scale; division of labor is efficient; and, therefore, specialized economies form and persist because the arrangement is efficient. Adam Smith, for one, believed this.
>
> The argument has two major flaws. In the first place, the reasoning is circular. It assumes that a result—in this case, efficiency—is its own cause. One might as well say that rain is beneficial to plants and that that is why it rains. The second flaw in the argument is that specialized economies are not efficient in any case. That is why they are commonly poor or else subsidized. To be sure, their specialties are sometimes (not always) efficiently produced. But that is not the same as saying these economies are efficient. An economy that contains few different niches for people's differing skills, interests, and imaginations is not efficient. An economy that is unresourceful and unadaptable is not efficient. An economy that can fill few of the needs of its own people and producers is not efficient.   —JANE JACOBS

32
THE PARAGRAPH

The primary purpose for using paragraphs is to make writing readily understandable to the reader. In modern writing, each new paragraph alerts the reader to expect a change—a new idea, a new approach to an idea, or further information about an idea. Occasionally, a new paragraph begins simply to break up a long expanse of prose. The length of a paragraph varies according to whether it appears in newspapers or magazines (short paragraphs) or in more formal kinds of writing such as essays and encyclopedia articles (longer paragraphs).

Approached from another perspective, the need to make paragraphs unified, coherent, and well developed helps the writer explore and shape ideas. In fact, lapses in unity and coherence often reflect lapses in thinking. The patterns of arrangement discussed in Section **32** aid in displaying ideas clearly. Derived from Aristotle's topics of invention, these methods of paragraph development often serve to generate ideas—the purpose for which Aristotle intended them.

Because students have difficulty understanding coherence, it is useful to begin by discussing various kinds of relationships—coordinate (*and*), obversative (*but*), alternative (*or*), causative (*because, for*), conclusive (*so*), inclusive (*colon*). (See also W. Ross Winterowd, "The Grammar of Coherence," *Contemporary Rhetoric: A Conceptual Background with Readings,* [New York: Harcourt, 1975].) The discussion might move to the ways of developing coherence described in **32b**—repetition of key words and ideas, repetition of pronouns, parallel structures, and use of transitional expressions. Finally, instructors may wish to discuss coherence as the set of relationships made explicit by the ordering and arrangement of sentences within a paragraph—that is, the relationships that go beyond the sentence.

ACTIVITIES

1. Ask students to think for five minutes about a recent experience and to jot on a piece of paper as many of the ideas and details that come to mind as possible. These jottings will probably be phrases or even single words; students should make no attempt at this point to structure sentences or to organize the material in any way. After the five minutes is up, ask students to create unified groups from the jottings and to structure as many sentences as necessary to include all of the points in each group. When that activity is completed, have students write a paragraph based on the sentences; ask them to use the coherence techniques in **32c** to make the relationships among the sentences clear.

   A variation on this activity is useful to teach the value of various methods of development. Begin the activity in the same way, but have the students jot any concrete, sensory details that come to mind—how someone or something looked, sounds they heard, smells they remember, tastes, textures. Then ask them to create unified groups of details and write one paragraph about each group. Any method of development (or combination of methods) that works for the material can be used as a principle for grouping—classification, comparison-contrast, narration, and so on.

2. Have the class suggest sentences following the patterns listed below. Then have each student write a paragraph developing that sentence.

   a. A sentence stating what someone might have learned from an experience or how someone feels about an experience.
   b. A sentence stating a fact or opinion.
   c. A sentence stating a subject that has several parts.
   (This activity adapted from Erika Lindemann, *A Rhetoric for Writing Teachers* [New York: Oxford UP, 1982].)

3. Ask students to evaluate the unity of one of their paragraphs by justifying the function of every sentence in the paragraph.

4. Have students analyze one of their essays to discover which categories of transitions are most frequently used and which, if any, are not used or are used infrequently. Have students share their analyses with the class. Ask students to compare their use of coherence strategies with those of other students and, if possible, with those of a professional writer.

5. Bring to class copies of two or three student paragraphs. In each, label the ways coherence is gained (by pronouns, key words, transitions, or parallel structure). Then ask students to analyze a paragraph they have written recently and revise it to improve unity.

6. Distribute copies of a professionally written paragraph from which you have removed as many of the aids to coherence as you conveniently can. (You may have to rewrite the paragraph slightly to remove parallel structures and repetition of key words or ideas.) Discuss with the class how the paragraph could be given coherence. If time permits, have the students attempt a revision of the paragraph before showing them the original paragraph (an overhead projector is useful for this part of the activity, but you can distribute copies or read the paragraph to the students).

7. Distribute a sheet which contains at the top the first sentence of a paragraph and at the bottom the last sentence. Have students write a minimum of three sentences (and probably no more than five) to complete the paragraph. (This activity adapted from Erika Lindemann, *A Rhetoric for Writing Teachers* [New York: Oxford UP, 1982].)

8. In random order, type and number sentences from a student or profession-

ally written paragraph. Ask students to determine what the proper order should be and explain why. Then read the original paragraph.

9. Have students isolate coherence chains (see paragraph 21, pp. 322–23) in one of their own paragraphs. Ask them to revise where necessary.

10. Have students collect paragraphs to illustrate the common arrangements of ideas discussed in **32b(1)**. Ask them to identify the topic sentence or controlling idea of each paragraph.

11. Select one topic sentence from each student's essay. Ask students what question(s) implied in the topic sentence must be answered in the development of the paragraph.

12. To demonstrate that description is based on observation and that powers of observation vary, during the final fifteen minutes of class burn a scented pillar candle—one that has been used several times before so that it will have an interesting shape. Have students describe the candle (ask them to write a list of fifty observations, but settle for twenty-five or so). Before the next class, type up the observations paragraph-style to save space. Ask students to compare the differences, thus opening a discussion of perception or of objective and subjective description.

13. To emphasize the use of criteria in classifying objects into parallel, non-overlapping categories, bring to class an apparently random assortment of silverware (knives, forks, teaspoons, sugar spoons, serving spoons, pickle forks, steak knives, stainless, silverplate, plastic, and so on). Ask students to group items according to function, material, pattern, finish.

ANSWERS TO EXERCISES

■ **Exercise 1** (p. 314)   **Unity in paragraphs**

Delete "It was very cold . . . late July" and "One day we saw . . . rocks."

■ **Exercise 5** (p. 326)   **Coherence in paragraphs**

Answers will vary. Here is a possible solution.

Cable television isn't the bargain it appears to be. Although reception is clear and all the local channels can be piped in to a television set for a relatively low cost per month, in most places subscribers have to pay as much as thirty dollars a month extra to receive such desirable channels as Home Box Office, Showtime, and Cinemax. A connection to a second or third television set also costs extra. Furthermore, the pay-TV movie channels run the same films over and over during a month's time, and many of the films are box office flops or re-runs of old movies that can be viewed on regular channels.

33

THE WHOLE COMPOSITION

This section emphasizes writing as a process. The rules, although presented as if they were a sequence of steps, represent the parts of a process and are interdependent. Students—usually product oriented—should be encouraged to move freely among the various parts and to examine their own composing habits in light of the steps presented here.

The rules stress the importance of planning, arrangement, and revision. The discussions of how to determine purpose, select a subject, and analyze an audience help students plan effectively. Students should be encouraged to modify the plans they make as they discover new directions and relationships.

The discussions concerning arrangement encourage students to use development strategies as a means to more coherent writing and explain the importance and function of clear thesis statements and effective introductions and conclusions.

The discussion of revision emphasizes both large-scale revision (clarifying, restructuring, deleting, or adding ideas as meanings emerge) and small-scale revision (editing sentences; correcting errors in spelling, mechanics, punctuation, and grammar). Students often resist revising, perhaps because revising papers that have already been graded seems futile. When they do revise, they rarely concern themselves with more than "a thesaurus philosophy of writing" (Nancy Sommers, "Revision Strategies of Student Writers and Experienced Writers," *College Composition and Communication* 31[Dec. 1980]: 381), tinkering with words rather than with ideas. Students can be encouraged to develop the revision approach that experienced writers use; in particular, they need to consider their purpose and the reader's expectations, and to work toward making the relationships among their ideas clear. As Sommers notes, "experienced writers explained that they get closer to the meaning by not limiting themselves too early to lexical concerns" (386). Since Section **33** encourages students to revise for clarity of ideas (one hallmark of an experienced writer) rather than revising individual words by simply substituting, omitting, or adding words, the student paper is presented in two forms. The first shows the paper undergoing revision, and the second shows the product.

Many of Strobeck's revisions are stylistic, eliminating wordy passages, improving diction, and the like. Notice particularly the revision of the introductory paragraph. Many revisions, however, involve larger issues such as improving focus and organization. For example, Strobeck's revision of the third paragraph turns his simile, "Some birds act like realtors," into a controlling metaphor for the entire paragraph. Furthermore, Strobeck's deletions frequently indicate how he clarifies ideas and makes the relationships between them clear. Deleting the final sentence of paragraph 4 makes his point more emphatic. Removing the cliché that introduces paragraph 5 allows Strobeck to compress his comparison of bird courtship and human love-life into a single, effective sentence that then works well with his description of the female martin's behavior. The deletion of the entire ninth paragraph removes a problem with focus: the references to refugees and starving hunters are inappropriate in an essay focused on family life. Strobeck's revision of the first sentence of his concluding paragraph provides good transition and sharpens the focus of the essay at the same time that it signals the conclusion. The revision of his concluding sentence contributes to clarity of ideas as well as to stylistic consistency. Alluding to the rainbow (from "My Heart Leaps Up") rather than to the daffodils (from "I Wandered Lonely as a Cloud"), Strobeck retains his focus on the sky—appropriate in an essay on birds. Notice also that Strobeck makes a further revision between his draft and his final copy, changing "to get rid of garbage—the droppings—" to "to dispose of household garbage, carrying away the droppings."

Writing answers to essay examinations (**33i**) is a kind of "'writing by formula.' Writing-by-formula is also necessary in college . . . [for] when writing under pressure, students who command a repertoire of formulas for organizing answers to essay exams save time" (Erika Lindemann, *A Rhetoric for Writing Teachers* [New York: Oxford UP, 1982]: 166). When discussing the essay test, a good strategy is to review methods of paragraph development by analyzing essay examination questions from various fields (such as psychology, textiles, child development, nursing, physics, literature, music, engineering). Explain that regardless of students' knowledge of the subject, they can structure an answer. The students' first task is to identify the type(s) of development implied by the questions. Then they can employ formulas for organizing the answers.

ACTIVITIES

1. After students have written an essay, ask them to list in chronological order and in as much detail as possible all of the steps that they went through as they wrote. Use their lists to introduce the concept of writing as a process: Which part of the process is the most difficult? Which is the easiest? Which are students most likely to rush through?

2. Ask students how they think professional writers differ from them in work habits, interests, and background.

3. Ask students whether there is any truth in the following statements:

   a. Good writing is spontaneous and natural.
   b. The essay is a form of writing that is not used much any more.
   c. Essays are usually equated with dull information.
   d. Students' essays should be written to please the instructor.
   e. As long as the ideas are clear, grammar and spelling are relatively unimportant.

4. Ask students to analyze several short articles to determine whether the

purpose of each is expressive, informative, or persuasive. Have them explain what clues they used to determine the purpose. If an article has more than one purpose, have students explain which purpose is dominant and why. Since students will probably refer to audience when explaining purpose, the interdependence of the steps in the process can readily be emphasized.

5. Ask students to select a subject employing the suggestions in **33b**. Then have them explore the subject using the strategies in **33d**: listing, questioning, applying perspectives, surveying development strategies. This activity also works well as a class discussion.

6. Have students compare articles on the same or similar topics written for a specialized and for a general audience. They might, for example, select an article from a professional journal in their field and then look for a comparable topic in a popular magazine. If they are unfamiliar with appropriate journals, have them ask their instructors.

7. Have students write on the board their thesis statements for the next theme. Analyze every statement for clarity and adequately narrowed subject. Ask students what the strengths and weaknesses of each statement are and have them suggest improvements. Ask them to submit a revised thesis at the next class meeting.

8. Have students collect examples of different strategies for opening paragraphs (quotation, rhetorical question, anecdote, example, statistics, or a combination of these) and then rewrite one of the opening paragraphs using a different strategy or combination of strategies.

9. Type up the first sentence from each student's introduction. Discuss the effectiveness of the sentences in gaining an audience's attention.

10. After students have completed an essay, ask them to write a sentence outline of it as a way to check the sequence and importance of ideas.

11. Have students begin revising by using peer-editing techniques. Peer editing can be done by simply having students exchange papers and, using the Reviser's Checklist (pp. 386–88) write comments upon their classmates' work, or it can be done by dividing the class into small groups and having students give an oral critique (this approach works best if students bring several copies of their draft to class).

Peer-editing is useful because it enables students to see that others have problems similar to their own, and because students are usually better critics of others' writing than of their own. Peer-editing gives them practice in seeing which questions to ask and what to look for. However, it should not be attempted without preparing the class and providing well-defined guidelines.

a. Make sure students know exactly what they are looking for. Early editing sessions are perhaps best limited to working with a single paragraph—perhaps the introduction. Later sessions can focus on the structure of the entire draft. Some classes will be deft enough to work on style toward the end of the term.

b. Stress that the criticism should be constructive, beginning with strengths and taking the student writer's stated intent into consideration. Weaknesses should be pointed out but the student critic should try to explain why a given point is a weakness and how to fix it.

c. Outline a procedure for editing. For instance, tell students to read quickly through a draft and jot a brief note about what they expect to find in each paragraph. Then have them read the paper more carefully, considering (1) thesis, (2) unity, (3) coherence, (4) arrangement, (5) conclusion, if any. Then have students write a comment noting what they found to be the main strong points and the main weak points in the paper.

34

THE RESEARCH PAPER

Students often perceive the research paper as altogether different from or more important than their other writing assignments. Instead of recognizing that the same process operates in both—defining, shaping, collecting, and revising—they concentrate on collecting information. Students may divorce writing a research paper from writing essays for several reasons:

1. A research paper is longer and more formal than an essay.
2. It is given more class time and more time for writing than any other essay.
3. It requires conventional research format (formal outline, citations, lists of works cited).
4. It is the type of essay most often required in other classes.
5. It is weighted more heavily in the final grade than any other essay.

With this perception, students tend to fall into the trap of budgeting most of their time for research, relatively little for writing, and almost none for revising. Losing sight of the composing process, the students rely heavily on conventions of format to carry their ideas. You can help students balance their attention to the steps in the process by reviewing each of the rules in Section **33** in terms of the research paper, by helping students to invent subjects, and by allowing time for revision after a conference on the second draft. Thus, by commenting on the entire process and by including time for revision, you can help students eliminate overemphasis of a single aspect.

After planning adequate time for each step, announce the schedule of deadlines for the unit. At the same time, announce your policy on late papers and missed conferences so that students have a clear understanding of what is expected of them from the outset.

If you assign works of literature as subjects for a research paper, here are a few cautions:

1. Do not assume that students possess the skills to read literature critically. They need help to understand a literary work so that their inexperience in interpreting literature does not unfairly hamper their ability to write a good essay.
2. Show them how list-making, the journalist's questions, and the three kinds of writing (**33d**) can be applied to literary terms in order to produce a topic.
3. Place on library reserve copies of the most important articles and books so that students have equal access to them.
4. Select at least three or four works—all, preferably, by different authors—to relieve the strain on the library's resources and to appeal to a variety of interests and reading abilities.
5. To avoid students' relying on *Masterplots* or *Readers' Guide* for their

information, you may want to distribute a list of bibliographic resources (with call numbers if possible) for students' use.

Whatever the subject of their research papers, students should be aware that the papers must do more than simply report general information. Unlike high-school research papers, college-level papers require something beyond what is included in encyclopedia entries. Although students may want to read them for background information, encyclopedias are not adequate resources for a research project.

You might suggest that when students take information from a journal or magazine they note on the bibliography card whether the source uses continuous or separate pagination. Thus, the students are prepared ahead of time to write these particular endnotes or footnotes in accurate form.

It is useful to stress that direct quotation should be used sparingly, and that long direct quotations are generally ineffective. Students will themselves admit that they generally skip over long direct quotations they encounter in their reading. Skillful use of summary and paraphrase, however, are among the most difficult techniques for students to master. Showing a few examples of summaries and paraphrases that have been seamlessly worked into the writer's own text can help, but students need to practice to develop the skill. (See Activity 3.) A useful distinction can be made between attribution (phrases such as *Brown says, Heller assumes, Jefferson insisted*) and documentation (the parenthetical author and/or page citation). Where necessary, attributive statements can be used, but it is usually better for students to try to integrate the information into their own prose and then cite the source. Otherwise, the paper assumes a scrapbook quality.

A candid discussion of plagiarism and its penalty informs the student and protects the instructor. In explaining the various kinds, be sure to stress the writer's responsibility for quoting accurately, paraphrasing carefully, and acknowledging honestly all of the sources cited. Students understand that copying sentences verbatim without proper documentation and passing another student's paper off as their own are examples of plagiarism. However, they usually do not know that misrepresenting the facts of publication, paraphrasing without a citation, or duplicating the order of another writer's examples are also examples of plagiarism. Tell the students to bring the original source as well as their use of it to you if they have any doubts about their use of materials. Thus, they can have troublesome summaries or paraphrases evaluated before they write the final draft of their paper.

As part of the research-paper unit, student-instructor conferences allow you to offer specific suggestions during the writing process, and these conferences benefit both you and the student by focusing on writing. The students prepare for the conference by writing whatever is required, making a list of questions to ask, and arriving on time. You prepare by signing up students for conference times, and by making a checklist of items to comment on. (Since a day of fifteen-minute conferences is exhausting, you should also schedule a break or two.) The students come away satisfied that their papers have been improved; you are reassured that students are writing their own papers.

ACTIVITIES

1. During the first class meeting of the semester, include some questions about the students' experience with research papers: how many, if any, they have written; for which courses; on what subjects. When, later in the semester, students select subjects for their research papers, you may choose to disallow areas in which the student has already written a paper.

2. Ask students to write a paraphrase and a summary for one passage you have chosen for the purpose. In a class where the research paper topics cover a number of areas, you might hand out a passage from an article in the area of most of the papers or use a paragraph from the essay anthology used in class. In a class where a literary topic has been assigned, you could choose a passage from a critical work—in a paper on *Nineteen Eighty-Four,* for example, one of the items mentioned in the bibliography for the model research paper in Section **34**. Or, if the students are using a standard sourcebook, such as Irving Howe's *Orwell's* Nineteen Eighty-Four: *Text, Sources, Criticism,* 2nd ed. (New York: Harcourt, 1982), you could simply ask them to turn to a passage you have chosen.

   Have students write their paraphrases and summaries on the board for analysis. Review the rules for the ellipsis mark (**17i**); then ask students to quote the passage directly in a way that requires the ellipsis mark. Have students write their sentence on the board; ask others to make any corrections necessary.

3. Collect several examples of sources seamlessly integrated into a writer's text. (You could use samples from your own or your colleagues' writing, from well-written journal articles, and from publications such as *Smithsonian, National Geographic, Science 86.*) Using an overhead projector to display the writings, discuss the techniques used. Then pass out sample informative paragraphs and ask students to write three or four sentences for each in which they integrate paraphrase and summary with their own ideas. Next, have students write a couple of sentences using attributive statements. Finally, have them write a couple of sentences in which they use brief direct quotations from the sources.

4. Bring to class photocopies of title pages and copyright pages for several books (or reproduce them from an overhead projector). Ask students which information belongs in a bibliographic entry and in what order. Then have them write the entry. (**Note:** Select material carefully to avoid such complications as identifying tags (for example, *former ambassador to the United Nations*), subtitles, and copyright pages with both printing dates and copyright dates.)

5. Ask students to bring to class their working bibliographies, at least six blank 3 × 5-inch cards, and a rubber band or large paper clip. Then select five sources from each student's bibliography, aiming for as much variety

as possible—a journal article, a book with two editions, an essay in an anthology, a multivolume work, and so on. Each student writes the proper bibliographic form on one side of a card and the proper footnote form on the other. To hand in the cards, students arrange them in proper bibliographical order. Two students using the same source but producing different entries should have an opportunity to compare and correct forms. (**Note:** This exercise has the advantage of testing students' ability to use the forms with sources that they will eventually include in the list of works cited.)

6. Arrange for students to tour the university library. If there is an opportunity to consult with the staff members who conduct the tours, explain what subjects students have selected and ask that appropriate reference tools be pointed out. Give students a list of questions to ask about library facilities and reference tools. The questions should correlate with students' subjects, and any questions not answered by the librarian's presentation should be asked by someone in the class. These questions might include

   a. What classification system is used for books that circulate?
   b. What is the difference between an abstract and an index?
   c. Where is the most convenient place to check the call number of a book listed in the *Essay and General Literature Index?*
   d. Once I have located an article in an index, where do I look to see whether or not the library has the journal in which it appears?
   e. Where is the Minneapolis *Tribune* [or a similar major regional newspaper] index located?
   f. What is the library's policy on students' reshelving books?
   g. If I know both the author and the title of a book, which card catalog would I go to first and why?

35

BUSINESS WRITING

While this section is devoted to business letters and résumés, memos, and reports, it also provides an opportunity to review all of the elements of clear, effective writing. Business writing must accomplish its purpose in relatively few words (usually one typed page or less). Thus, every word must contribute to the message without confusing or offending the reader.

Four of the elements to review include

1. *Formulating and developing a thesis.* Because "time is money," a business person wants to know immediately why the letter was written and what action, if any, the writer expects. The opening paragraph contains the thesis, which is developed by careful explanation and relevant details in the body paragraphs. The concluding paragraph should state who does what next.

2. *Analyzing an audience.* Here the writer should consider how the addressee will react. Will he or she be pleased by the request (an order for camping gear), irritated (a demand that certain repairs be made to an apartment before the rent is paid), or both (a rush shipment of bayberry candles the week before Christmas)? If the response is likely to be at least in part negative, the writer should organize the letter so that the reader is not overpowered by the negative elements. The tone should be neither insulting nor patronizing.

3. *Diction.* Clear, exact words convey precise images (a *Zenith 19-inch portable color television, model number 194467792,* instead of *my new color television*). As much as possible, avoid such phrases as *time frame* or *analyzation of invoiced goods as per your aforementioned authorization* which are not only imprecise and therefore inefficient, but also boring.

4. *Mechanics and spelling.* Readers of business prose expect standard spelling and mechanics; anything less creates a negative impression. It goes without saying that the addressee's and company's names must be spelled correctly. In letters of application and résumés especially, accuracy is imperative; more résumés are eliminated for reasons of sloppiness and misspelling than for any other.

Students who are applying for jobs should be advised to prepare their résumés before writing letters of application. Writing a résumé should not be a hurried affair. For each of the four major sections students should answer several questions as they collect and organize material:

Personal data

1. How should I give my name (no nicknames)?
2. Is it necessary to include both my school address and my home address? If so, what format should I use?

Suggested Format:

Diane Bellows

Until May 20, 1981	After May 20, 1981
1830 Lexington Avenue	2158 Claussen Trail
Louisville, KY 40227	West Lafayette, IN 47906
(502) 698–3137	(317) 712–8798

Educational background

1. What is the formal name of the school(s) I have attended? (for example, The Pennsylvania State University, not Penn State)
2. What degree(s) did I earn?
3. What are the dates during which I attended?
4. What was my major? minor?
5. What was my grade-point average overall? in my major? in my minor?
6. What advanced seminars or research projects have I taken that are related to the job(s) for which I am applying?
7. What academic honors did I earn?
8. What professional organizations did I join? What offices or committee memberships did I hold? When? What were the responsibilities of each position I held?
9. What social organizations did I join?

Work experience

1. What jobs—including volunteer work—have I held?
2. What were the dates of employment for each job?
3. What was the job title for each position?
4. What was the name of the company for whom I worked?
5. Who was my supervisor or boss?
6. What were my responsibilities?

Location of credentials file

1. What is the official title and address of the Placement Office?
2. What is the telephone number of the Placement Office?
3. Which employers and professors should I ask for letters of recommendation? How many letters should I have in my file?
4. How can I judge who will write the most effective letter?
5. What is the correct procedure for requesting a letter?

6. How soon should I check to see whether my file contains all of the necessary letters?
7. What should I do if a letter has not been sent yet?

After the information has been collected, the student should write each section (obviously not all of the information is necessarily included; a low grade-point average, for example, is better omitted), making it complete but concise (*wrote press releases* instead of *my responsibilities included writing press releases*). Then the student should consider the arrangement of the sections on the page. Personal data and references are placed first and last, respectively. Education is usually placed second, but those whose employment experience is stronger than their educational preparation may want to place the employment section second. In any event, the students should experiment with the use of spacing, capitalization, and underlining until they discover a format that adequately emphasizes their strengths.

Only after students have completed their résumés should they attempt a letter of application. Having analyzed their background and that of the company, they can better match their strengths with the requirements listed in the job description.

Like other business letters, the application letter follows a thesis-development-action structure, with the applicant's most persuasive qualifications offered on a single page. The first paragraph tells how the applicant learned of the job and why he or she is qualified for it by education and experience; the central strengths are identified at the outset. The second paragraph develops the education section of the thesis (including, perhaps, any research projects or seminars that are directly related to the position and that may or may not be included on the résumé). The third develops work experiences related to the position or to the qualities desired for the position. The concluding paragraph requests an interview. To discover more about the candidate than the one-page letter allows, the reader then refers to the résumé.

ACTIVITIES

1. Ask students to bring to class two business letters and two memos. Students may use ones they have received or, with permission, ones from their jobs. Have them work in small groups to analyze the format (the placement of the parts), the structure (thesis, development, action), spelling, and neatness of each. Ask students how their analyses affect their opinions of the company.

2. Suggest that students attend any résumé or interviewing workshop held by the Placement Office.

3. Ask someone from the Placement Office to talk to the class about the résumés students in the class have written. The instructor should submit

copies well in advance so that the speaker can plan his or her comments and arrange for any necessary visual aids.

4. Ask students to write a letter requesting a letter of recommendation.

5. Invite the person in charge of hiring for a local business to share suggestions for an effective résumé.

6. Have students interview employers to discover the essentials of an effective letter and résumé as far as that company is concerned.

CRITERIA FOR EVALUATING AND GRADING THEMES

Knowing what letter grades symbolize helps both the instructor and the students. The instructor who adheres to clearly defined criteria (especially if the criteria are in use throughout the department) can concentrate on specific comments about the students' organization, development, and style rather than defend both the criteria and the comments every time a set of essays is returned. Students who understand that the criteria are a ready checklist as they revise also know that the degree to which the criteria are satisfied determines their grade; thus, they are confident of consistent standards from theme to theme. Finally, the use of such standards as those presented here makes clear the point that merely meeting the requirements of the assignment does not guarantee an A.

The following criteria deal with subject matter, style, use of rhetorical modes, organization, development, and mechanics. The final sentences of the A, B, and C paragraphs succinctly point out the differences in quality.*

A paper: Perhaps the principal characteristic of the A paper is its rich content. Some people describe the content as "meaty," others as "dense," still others as "packed." Whatever, the A paper demonstrates an excellent command of the subject matter. The information delivered is such that one feels significantly taught by the author, sentence after sentence, paragraph after paragraph. The A paper is also marked by stylistic finesse: the title and the opening paragraph are engaging; the transitions are artful; the phrasing is tight, fresh, and highly specific; the sentence structure is varied; the tone enhances the purpose of the paper. The A paper shows an ability to explain, illustrate, compare, contrast, and synthesize ideas; it is consistently and adequately appropriate. Finally, the A paper, because of its careful organization and development, imparts a feeling of wholeness and unusual clarity. Not surprisingly, then, it leaves the reader

---

*These grading criteria were written by John Trimble of the Department of English, The University of Texas, Austin, and are reprinted by permission.

feeling bright, thoroughly satisfied, and eager to reread the piece. In short, the A paper is organized, clear, coherent, and effective throughout.

B paper: It is significantly more than competent. Besides being almost free of mechanical errors, the B paper delivers substantial information—that is, substantial in both quantity and interest. It demonstrates a good knowledge of the subject matter as well as a capacity for fluency of ideas and independent thinking, although not always realized in the paper. The specific points are logically ordered, well developed, and unified around a clear organizing principle that is apparent early in the paper. The ideas are usually adequately supported. The opening paragraph draws the reader in; the closing paragraph is both conclusive and thematically related to the opening. The transitions between paragraphs are for the most part smooth, the sentence structures pleasingly varied. The diction of the B paper is typically much more concise and precise than that found in the C paper. Occasionally, it even shows distinctiveness—i.e., finesse and memorability. On the whole, then, a B paper makes the reading experience a pleasurable one, for it offers substantial information with few distractions. In short, the writing in the B paper is organized, clear, coherent, and correct.

C paper: It is generally competent—it meets the assignment, has few mechanical errors, and is reasonably well organized and developed. The C paper demonstrates an average knowledge of the subject matter. The actual information it delivers, however, seems thin and commonplace. One reason for that impression is that the ideas are typically cast in the form of vague generalities— generalities that prompt the reader to ask marginally: "In every case?" "Exactly how large?" "Why?" "But how many?" The C paper reveals a weakness in effectively stating, explaining, and discussing ideas; the paper tends to be static—it does not "go anywhere." Stylistically, the C paper has other shortcomings as well: the opening paragraph does little to draw the reader in; the final paragraph offers only a perfunctory wrap-up; the transitions between paragraphs are often bumpy; the sentences, besides being choppy, tend to follow a predictable (hence monotonous) subject-verb-object order; the diction is occasionally marred by unconscious repetitions, redundancy, and imprecision. The C paper, then, while it accomplishes its purpose, lacks both imagination and intellectual rigor, and hence does not invite a rereading. The writing in the C paper is clear, controlled, and correct for the most part, but expression is occasionally faulty.

D paper: Its treatment and development of the subject are only rudimentary; the D paper demonstrates an inadequate grasp of the subject matter and fails to state, discuss, and develop ideas effectively. Ideas are inadequately supported. While organization is present, it is neither clear nor effective. Sentences are frequently awkward, ambiguous, and marred by serious mechanical errors. The writing is faulty: errors occur in mechanics (spelling, punctuation, run-on sentences, sentence fragments, subject-verb or pronoun-antecedent agreement), phrasing (awkward, unidiomatic, or ungrammatical sentences, inaccurate or inappropriate diction), organization (lack of paragraph logic, development, or unity). Evidence of careful proofreading is scanty, if it exists at all. In fact, the whole paper often gives the impression of having been conceived and written in haste.

F **paper:** Its treatment of the subject is superficial; its theme lacks discernible organization; its prose is garbled or stylistically primitive. The F paper manifests any or all of the qualities of the D theme. Errors in mechanics are frequent. The F paper fails to follow or to complete an assignment. In short, the ideas, organization, and style fall far below what is acceptable college writing.

SUGGESTED READINGS ON COMPOSITION

The results of research in the teaching of writing, both theory and application, are regularly found in the following journals. (An asterisk indicates a journal that publishes bibliographies of significant current articles.)

Basic Writing
College English Association Forum
Conference on Language Attitudes and Composition (*CLAC*)
College Composition and Communication
College English
English Education
English Journal
Freshman English News
Language Arts
Research in the Teaching of English
Rhetoric Society Quarterly
Style
Teaching English in the Two-Year College
Writing as a Liberating Activity Newsletter

Throughout this bibliography the bracketed numbers refer to related sections in the *Harbrace College Handbook.* An asterisk precedes titles that are considered required reading for all teachers of composition.

BIBLIOGRAPHIES AND BIBLIOGRAPHICAL ESSAYS

Bennett, James R., et al. "The Paragraph: An Annotated Bibliography." *Style* 11 (Spring 1977): 107–18. • Includes references on structure, the process of paragraphing, and the relation of the paragraph to the entire work. [**32**]
Cooper, Charles R., and Lee Odell, eds. *Research on Composing: Points of*

Departure. Urbana: NCTE, 1978. • An anthology that includes selections by such researchers as Janet Emig, James Britton, and Donald Murray.

Dieterich, Daniel J., and Richard H. Behm. "Annotated Bibliography of Research in the Teaching of English." *Research in the Teaching of English.* • Appearing twice yearly in the May and December issues, the bibliography annotates research in bilingual/bidialectal studies; language and verbal learning; literature, humanities, and media; teacher education; testing and evaluation; written and oral communication. Bibliographies prior to 1979 are written by Dieterich.

Gorrell, Robert M., Patricia Bizzell, and Bruce Herzberg, eds. *Bedford Bibliography for Teachers of Writing.* Boston: Bedford, 1983. • Annotated bibliography of articles on all aspects of the composing process.

Larson, Richard L. "Selected Bibliography of Research and Writing About the Teaching of Composition." *College Composition and Communication.* • Annual annotated bibliography first published in May 1975.

———. "Selected Bibliography of Writings on the Evaluation of Students' Achievements in Composition." *Journal of Basic Writing* 1 (Spring–Summer 1978): 91–100. • Annotations of articles focused on evaluating or responding to students' writing.

Tate, Gary, ed. *Teaching Composition: Ten Bibliographical Essays.* Fort Worth: Texas Christian UP, 1976. • A collection of essays on topics central to the teaching of writing. Includes essays on invention, structure and form, style, modes of discourse, basic writing, uses of media, linguistics, rhetorical analysis, dialects, and fields related to composition.

THEORY

Beach, Richard, and Lillian S. Bridwell. *New Directions in Composition Research.* New York: Guilford, 1984. • Twenty essays survey research methods, the composing process, the writing situation, and the instructional context.

Britton, James, et al. *The Development of Writing Abilities (11–18).* London: Collier Macmillan, 1975. • Reports on research project; bases a classification system of writing on both function and audience.

D'Angelo, Frank. *A Conceptual Theory of Rhetoric.* Cambridge: Winthrop, 1975. • Proposes a theory of linguistic and rhetorical principles that "determine the intrinsic nature of discourse." Context and essential characteristics of rhetoric examined in an effort to "explore the relationships that exist between thinking and writing, within the framework of a coherent theoretical system of rhetoric."

Emig, Janet. "Writing as a Mode of Learning." *College Composition and Communication* 28 (May 1977): 122–28. • Contends writing is a "unique mode of learning" and contrasts writing with talking. Outlines parallels between writing and successful learning strategies. **[33]**

* Hirsch, E. D., Jr. *The Philosophy of Composition.* Chicago: U of Chicago P,

1977. • Believes readability should be the major stylistic concern in both teaching and evaluation. Chapter 6 ("Some Practical Implications") offers suggestions to improve teaching methods.
* Kinneavy, James L. *A Theory of Discourse.* Englewood Cliffs: Prentice, 1971. • Detailed, systematic study of reference, persuasive, literary, and expressive discourse. [**33**]
* Moffett, James. *Teaching the Universe of Discourse.* Boston: Houghton, 1968. • Discussion of the author's discourse theory based on speaker, audience, and subject. Shows parallels between discourse and levels of abstraction. Drama and narrative discourse examined in particular detail. Points out the strengths and weaknesses of transformational grammar, sentence combining, and textbooks. [**32, 33**]
* Winterowd, W. Ross, ed. *Contemporary Rhetoric: A Conceptual Background with Readings.* New York: Harcourt, 1975. • A collection of twenty-four essays on invention, form, and style. Interprets recent work on rhetoric and establishes the direction of future work. Introductory essay by the editor.

APPROACHES AND STRATEGIES

Coles, William. *Composing: Writing as a Self-Creating Process.* Rochelle Park: Hayden, 1974. • Presents thirty cases or problems.
———— . *The Plural I: The Teaching of Writing.* New York: Holt, 1978. • An account of how students in a composition class move from being students who write themes to writers who recognize the power of their voices.
* Corbett, Edward P. J. *Classical Rhetoric for the Modern Student.* 2nd ed. New York: Oxford UP, 1971. • Presents the three essential units of classical rhetoric: invention, arrangement, and style. Emphasizes argument.
D'Angelo, Frank. "Advertising and the Modes of Discourse." *College Composition and Communication* 29 (Dec. 1978): 356–61. • Examines ads as examples of descriptive, narrative, and expository-argumentative modes. Includes a checklist of six suggestions for using advertising to teach forms of discourse. [**33**]
Donovan, Timothy, and Ben W. McClelland, eds. *Eight Approaches to Teaching Composition.* Urbana: NCTE, 1980. • Collection that includes essays on rhetorical, epistemic, and revised-models approaches as well as essays on basic writing, conference, and across-the-curriculum approaches.
Elbow, Peter. *Writing Without Teachers.* New York: Oxford UP, 1975. • Focuses on invention in free writing; advises reader-writer how to benefit from the process of reacting to writing. Explains how to set up a "teacher-less" course.
Flower, Linda. *Problem-Solving Strategies for Writing.* New York: Harcourt, 1981. • Brings together the rhetorical topics (invention, arrangement, and style) and a process approach to writing in order to show how an awareness of intellectual processes affects a writer's strategies.

Griffin, C. Williams, ed. *New Directions for Teaching and Learning: Teaching Writing in All Disciplines*. No 12. San Francisco: Jossey, 1982. • Focused on writing-across-the-curriculum, this volume contains ten essays focused upon the theory behind writing-across-the-curriculum, writing as a cognitive process, writing as learning, the future of the movement, and resources available.

Graves, Richard L., ed. *Rhetoric and Composition: A Sourcebook for Teachers*. Rochelle Park: Hayden, 1976. • Anthology of articles from professional journals. Emphasis on motivating writers, teaching the sentence and the paragraph, using classical rhetoric. One section is devoted to techniques of teaching. Authors include Cooper, Christensen, Becker, Larson, Berthoff, Corbett, and Winterowd.

Hoffman, Eleanor M., and John P. Schifsky. "Designing Writing Assignments." *English Journal* 66 (Dec. 1977): 41–45. • Suggests that writing assignments should specify the aim, mode, audience, and purpose of the discourse. Three sets of satisfactory and unsatisfactory assignments are included. [**32, 33, 35**]

Irmscher, William F. *Teaching Expository Writing*. New York: Holt, 1979. • Practical guidance on organizing a course along with instruction on teaching mechanics, style, structure. Includes assignments and activities. Analyzes the qualities (content, form, diction, mechanics, and style) of A, B, and C essays with less attention to D and E essays.

Koch, Carl, and James M. Brazil. *Strategies for Teaching the Composition Process*. Urbana: NCTE, 1978. • Presents resources and strategies for a student-centered, process-oriented writing class. In addition to instructions for pre-writing, writing, and post-writing stages, the authors include a section on helping students overcome writing anxieties.

Lindemann, Erika. *A Rhetoric for Writing Teachers*. New York: Oxford UP, 1982. • A comprehensive guide to teaching writing as process. Exceptionally clear and concise discussions of composition theory are based on Kenneth Burke's ideas.

Macrorie, Ken. *Telling Writing*. Rochelle Park: Hayden, 1970. • A free-writing program in which students gain a knowledge of their own writing voices as well as the enthusiasm and ways of professional writers.

McKeachie, Wilbert J. *Teaching Tips: A Guide-Book for the Beginning College Teacher*. 7th ed. Lexington: Heath, 1978. • Discusses the how-to's of preparing to teach a course, meeting a class for the first time, leading discussion, and evaluating students' progress. Appendices include an evaluation form for teachers and a checklist of teaching techniques.

Murray, Donald M. *A Writer Teaches Writing: A Practical Method of Teaching Composition*. Boston: Houghton, 1968. • In addition to presenting a method of teaching composition, offers sample lesson plans and advice on designing and evaluating assignments. Myths of teaching composition, a collection of quotations from writers on writing, and an extensive bibliography of works for the teacher's library are also included.

Ohmann, Richard M., and W. B. Coley, eds. *Ideas for Teaching English 101: Teaching Writing in College*. Urbana: NCTE, 1975. • Reprints twenty-three articles from *College English*, Mar. 1967–Jan. 1975. Essays covering methods, theories, models, and suggestions are written by such authors as Bruffee, Winterowd, Wiener, Macrorie, Mandel, and Comprone.

Tate, Gary, and Edward P. J. Corbett. *The Writing Teacher's Sourcebook.* New York: Oxford UP, 1981. • Contains many of the basic articles for understanding current composition theory.

Winterowd, W. Ross. *The Contemporary Writer.* 2nd ed. New York: Harcourt, 1981. • Shows how much of the theory works out in classroom practice.

Young, Richard E., Alton L. Becker, and Kenneth L. Pike. *Rhetoric: Discovery and Change.* New York: Harcourt, 1970. • Discusses the making of choices in writing by applying six maxims derived from tagmemics. See Chapter 14 for a discussion of revision.

WRITING ABOUT LITERATURE [33, 34]

Roberts, Edgar V. *Writing Themes About Literature.* 4th ed. Englewood Cliffs: Prentice, 1977. • Specific guidelines for writing and organizing papers of summary, analysis (for example, character, point of view, structure, imagery, tone), evaluation, and review. Includes sample themes for each type of assignment.

Rohrberger, Mary, and Samuel H. Woods, Jr. *Reading and Writing About Literature.* New York: Random, 1971. • Provides context by introducing genre, critical approaches, and critical vocabulary. Discusses thesis, introductions, primary and secondary sources.

THE RESEARCH PAPER [34]

Katz, William. *Your Library: A Reference Guide.* 2nd ed. New York: Holt, 1984. • Explains to the beginning researcher how to use the library's resources and then how to locate sources in the humanities, science, social sciences. Useful charts key research questions to appropriate resources. Title index includes Library of Congress and Dewey Decimal numbers for every resource mentioned in the book.

Gibaldi, Joseph, and Walter S. Achtert. *MLA Handbook for Writers of Research Papers.* 2nd ed. New York: MLA, 1984. • Contains complete information on matters of format and parenthetical style of documentation recommended by MLA.

Turabian, Kate L. *A Manual for Writers of Term Papers, Theses, and Dissertations.* 4th ed. Chicago: U of Chicago P/Phoenix, 1973. • Manual of style for both scientific and nonscientific formal papers. Directions on format, organization, and mechanics of typing.

Winkler, Anthony C., and Jo Ray McCuen. *Writing the Research Paper: A Handbook.* 2nd ed. New York: Harcourt, 1985. • Includes annotated lists of general and specialized references as well as a guide to writing about literature.

ARGUMENTATION

Boley, Tommy J. "A Heuristic for Persuasion," *College Composition and Communication* 20 (May 1979): 187–91. • Contains a useful set of questions for invention.

Kneupper, Charles W. "Teaching Argument: An Introduction to the Toulmin Model." *College Composition and Communication* 29 (Oct. 1978): 237–41. • Explains the model of argument now used in speech instruction and applies it to paragraph one of Thoreau's "Civil Disobedience" to illustrate its usefulness in discourse analysis. The model consists of six elements: data, warrant, claim, qualifier, reservation, backing. [**33**]

Weddle, Perry. *Argument: A Guide to Critical Thinking.* New York: McGraw, 1977. • Seven chapters explaining and illustrating such subjects as fallacy, authority, cause, connotation, and definition. [**19, 31, 32**]

EVALUATION

Cooper, Charles R., and Lee Odell, eds. *Evaluating Writing: Describing, Measuring, Judging.* Urbana: NCTE, 1977. • Six essays on measuring and evaluating growth in writing plus an introduction by the editors. Topics include holistic scoring, syntactic maturity, and approaches to evaluation.

* Diederich, Paul B. *Measuring Growth in English.* Urbana: NCTE, 1974. • Outlines a system of staff grading; also includes topics for essay tests, a thirty-four–item test on knowledge of grammar, and a discussion on the harm of excessive correction.

Krishna, Valerie. "The Syntax of Error." *Journal of Basic Writing* 1 (Spring 1975): 43–49. • To help students overcome problems of illogical syntax, recommends having them locate main ideas in subjects and verbs. [**1, 24, 29**]

Lloyd-Jones, Richard. "Primary Trait Scoring." *Evaluating Writing: Describing, Measuring, Judging.* Ed. Charles R. Cooper and Lee Odell. Urbana: NCTE, 1977. 33–66. • Explains steps in primary trait scoring: defining the "universe of discourse" and developing exercises for it, securing the writers' cooperation, developing and using workable scoring guides. Two writing tasks along with their scoring guides illustrate the evaluation of students' discourse.

* Shaughnessy, Mina P. *Errors and Expectations: A Guide for the Teacher of Basic Writing.* New York: Oxford UP, 1977. • Analyzes range of writing problems, offers explanations for the occurrence of the problems, and suggests ways to handle the problems. Includes outlines of sample lessons, a sequence of lessons on verbs, and teaching activities. Discusses handwriting and punctuation, syntax, common errors, spelling, vocabulary, and elements beyond the sentence. Also provides a chart of writing skills to help in the planning of a composition sequence, an appendix of topics for placement essays, and an annotated bibliography.

THE PROCESS:
PREWRITING AND INVENTION

Adams, James L. *Conceptual Blockbusting: A Guide to Better Ideas.* San Francisco: Freeman, 1974. • The director of the Design Laboratory at Stanford University discusses problem-solving and heuristics in an accessible and interesting way.

Larson, Richard L. "Problem-Solving, Composing and Liberal Education." *College English* 33 (Mar. 1972): 628–35. • Applies eight steps of problem-solving to Swift's "A Modest Proposal" as part of a demonstration that problem-solving is a strategy for defining, organizing, and evaluating complex arguments. [**23, 32, 33**]

Phelps, Louise Wetherbee. "Dialectics of Coherence: Toward an Integrative Theory." *College English* 47 (Jan. 1985): 12–29. • Assesses the need for reintegration of process and product leading toward texts as "dynamic elements in a wonderfully intricate dance of discourse."

Brannon, Lil, Melinda Knight, and Vara Neverow-Turk. *Writers Writing.* Montclair: Boynton/Cook, 1982. • "Dramatization of the composing process" with comments from writers about how they write.

Berthoff, Ann E. *Forming/Thinking/Writing.* Rochelle Park: Hayden, 1979. • Offers approaches to help students become aware of and take control of their own writing processes.

Ede, Lisa, and Andrea Lunsford. "Audience Addressed/Audience Invoked: The Role of Audience in Composition Theory and Pedagogy." *College Composition and Communication* 35 (Feb. 1984): 155–72. • Expanded model of audience indicates the complexity of the writer's relation to and control of audience.

* Emig, Janet. *The Composing Processes of Twelfth Graders.* NCTE Research Report 13. Urbana: NCTE, 1971. • Reports on the case study of the composing processes used by eight twelfth-grade students. Finds that the characteristics of "self-sponsored" writing include peers as the selected audience, subjects from all fields, no "written prefiguring," stopping during the process, occasional contemplative pauses, and fairly ready revision. Behavior for "school-sponsored" writing, on the other hand, differs in the categories of context, stimuli, pre-writing, stopping, contemplation, and voluntary revision. [**32, 33**]

Flower, Linda, and John R. Hayes. "The Cognition of Discovery: Defining a Rhetorical Problem." *College Composition and Communication* 31 (Feb. 1980): 21–32. • Defines discovery as "an act of making meaning . . . in response to a *self-defined problem* or goal" and charts the elements of a rhetorical problem (rhetorical situation and writer's personal goals). Observes that good writers "respond to *all* aspects of the rhetorical problem," "create a particularly rich network of goals for affecting their reader," and "represent the problem not only in more breadth, but in depth." [**32, 33**]

———. "Problem-Solving Strategies and the Writing Process." *College English* 39 (Dec. 1977): 449–61. • Recommends problem-solving approach and outlines in detail a heuristic strategy for analytical writing. Notes that while the problem-solving approach does not yield ready-made steps to producing discourse, it does acknowledge the workings of the thought process. [**32, 33**]

Rohman, D. Gordon. "Pre-Writing: The Stage of Discovery in the Writing Process." *College Composition and Communication* 16 (May 1965): 106–12. • Suggests journals, principles of meditation, and analogy as ways to help students define a subject and a context for their writing. [**33**]

Rose, Mike. "Rigid Rules, Inflexible Plans, and the Stifling of Language: A Cognitivist Analysis of Writer's Block." *College Composition and Communication* 31 (Dec. 1980): 384–401. Offers a good discussion of writer's block.

THE PROCESS:
WRITING AND ARRANGEMENT [**31, 32**]

Baker, Sheridan. *The Practical Stylist.* 5th ed. New York: Crowell, 1980. • Begins with the thesis statement, moving then to paragraph structure and the sentence. Home of the "argumentative edge" and "funnel paragraph." With exercises.

Hartwell, Patrick. "Teaching Arrangement: A Pedagogy." *College English* (Jan. 1979): 548–54. • Outlines in detail a plan for teaching arrangement.

Larson, Richard L. "Toward a Linear Rhetoric of the Essay." *College Composition and Communication* 22 (May 1971): 140–46. • Argues for a linear plan to complement hierarchical models of discourse. The plan is based on five propositions: that the essay is made up of a series of steps, that "similar overall plans . . . organize many different essays," that an essay may include more than one plan, that the selection of a plan or plans influences the reader's reaction to the discussion, and that the selection of a plan or plans "probably determines in large part the data and materials."

Winterowd, W. Ross. "The Grammar of Coherence." *College English* 31 (May 1970): 828–35. • Argues that there is a grammar of coherent discourse and that the grammar is composed of seven relationships: coordination, obversativity, causativity, conclusivity, alternativity, inclusivity, and sequence.

THE PROCESS: STYLE

Joos, Martin. *The Five Clocks.* New York: Harcourt/Harbinger, 1967. • Introduction to the five styles of English: frozen, formal, consultative, casual, and intimate. [**19, 27, 33**]

Strunk, William, Jr., and E. B. White. *The Elements of Style.* 3rd ed. New York: Macmillan, 1978. • Four chapters concentrate on the most frequent errors of usage; in the fifth chapter White adds his views on style.

Williams, Joseph. *Style: Ten Lessons in Clarity and Grace.* Glenview: Scott,
     1981. • The single best work on accessibility (the relative readability of
     prose).

THE PROCESS: REVISION

Sommers, Nancy. "Revision Strategies of Student Writers and Experienced
     Adult Writers." *College Composition and Communication* 31 (Dec. 1980):
     378–88. • A case study using twenty student writers and twenty experi-
     enced writers shows that student writers view revising as a matter of re-
     wording. Students have strategies for the word and sentence levels but not
     for the essay as a whole. Experienced writers revise to define meaning
     and to meet the anticipated judgment of an audience; they have strategies
     for all levels and see revision as a recursive, holistic process. While stu-
     dents force their essays to meet narrowly defined rules given them by
     instructors, experienced writers create meaning as they write. [**20, 23, 25,
     29, 32, 33**]
Lanham, Richard A. *Revising Business Prose.* New York: Scribner's, 1981. •
     Lanham's eight-step Paramedic Method from *Revising Prose* (Scribner's,
     1978) applied to the prose of business and government. Section on Official
     Style includes Philip Broughton's "Systematic Buzz Phrase Projector."
     [**19, 21**]

DICTION AND USAGE

Algeo, John. *Problems in the Origins and Development of the English Lan-
     guage.* 3rd ed. New York: Harcourt, 1983. • Chapters 1 and 8 contain
     information on OED and early dictionaries. Examples of lexical and se-
     mantic change in Chapters 10 and 12. [**5, 7, 15, 19**]
Newman, Edwin. *Strictly Speaking: Will America Be the Death of English?*
     Indianapolis: Bobbs, 1974. • Uses many illustrations from politics, edu-
     cation, journalism, advertising, sports, and gastronomy to support the the-
     sis that language mirrors society and to argue for lucid English. [**19–21**]
Pyles, Thomas, and John Algeo. *The Origins and Development of the English
     Language.* 3rd ed. New York: Harcourt, 1983. • Systematically traces
     the phonological, grammatical, and syntactic changes in English. Chapters
     10 ("New Words from Old: Coinages and Adaptations") and 12 ("Words
     and Meanings") catalog methods of lexical and semantic change. [**19**]
Shuy, Roger W. *Discovering American Dialects.* Urbana: NCTE, 1967. •
     Brief general guide to the field of dialectology. Items and checklist of the
     phonology, grammar, and lexicon of regional dialects. [**19**]

THE SENTENCE

Christensen, Francis. "A Generative Rhetoric of the Sentence." *College Composition and Communication* 14 (Oct. 1963): 155–61. • Defines the four principles of a generative rhetoric of the sentence as addition, direction of movement, levels of generality or abstraction, and texture. Recommends Paul Roberts' *English Sentences* (Harcourt, 1962) as the grammar to clarify levels of syntax. Sees a shift in prose away from the complex sentence to the cumulative sentence. Examples included. [**1, 24, 25, 29, 30**]

Daiker, Donald, Andrew Kerek, and Max Morenberg. *The Writer's Options: College Sentence Combining.* New York: Harper, 1979. • Eighteen units of exercises designed to show students the varieties of structures (such as participles, absolutes, relative clauses) and strategies (such as emphasis, coherence, tone) available to writers. Also a chapter showing how a controlling idea (topic sentence) determines the content and organization of a paragraph. [**1, 25, 27, 29, 32**]

Graves, Richard L. "Levels of Skill in the Composing Process." *College Composition and Communication* 29 (Oct. 1978): 227–32. • Explains the mental processes involved in three progressively more complex activities: combining kernel sentences, revising flawed sentences, and composing sentences based on rhetorical models. [**24–26, 29, 30**]

Hunt, Kellogg W. *Grammatical Structures Written at Three Grade Levels.* NCTE Research Report 3. Champaign: NCTE, 1965. • Reports findings of a study on the writing of fifty-four students, each writing approximately one thousand words. Concludes that length of independent clauses (T-units) is related to maturity: the writing of adults contains longer T-units than those in twelfth graders' writing. [**24–26, 29, 30**]

———. *Syntactic Maturity in Schoolchildren and Adults.* Monographs of the Society for Research in Child Development 134. Chicago: U of Chicago P, 1970. • Reports findings of a study of writing done by more than one thousand students (grades 4, 6, 8, and 10) asked to rewrite the "aluminum passage," thirty-two short sentences. Finds that older students write longer T-units, use more strategies for revision, and add meanings as they revise. [**24–26, 29, 30**]

Mellon, John C. *Transformational Sentence-Combining: A Method for Enhancing the Development of Syntactic Fluency in English Composition.* NCTE Research Report 10. Champaign: NCTE, 1969. • Reports on a one-year experiment in which sentence-combining (without instruction in transformational rules) was taught as part of seventh graders' unit in linguistics; finds a significant increase in syntactic fluency. [**24–26, 29, 30**]

O'Hare, Frank. *Sentence Combining: Improving Student Writing Without Formal Grammar Instruction.* NCTE Research Report 15. Urbana: NCTE, 1973. • Reports growth in syntactic maturity of seventh graders when sentence-combining is taught without introducing the terminology of transformational grammar. [**24–26, 29, 30**]

Pence, R. W., and D. W. Emery. *A Grammar of Present-Day English.* 2nd ed. New York: Macmillan, 1963. • A detailed grammar of English using the traditional approach. [**1, 6, 7**]

Rippon, Michelle, and Walter E. Meyers. *Combining Sentences.* New York: Harcourt, 1979. • After a quick review of sentence types and parts of speech, thirty-four lessons give students abundant practice in combining with the use of simple signals and instructions. A final section is devoted to planning and writing a paragraph.

Roberts, Paul. *English Sentences.* New York: Harcourt, 1962. • Early transformational-generative grammar still useful for its classification of sentence patterns. [**1**]

Strong, William. "Sentence Combining: Back to the Basics and Beyond." *English Journal* 65 (Feb. 1976): 56, 60–64. • Stresses sentence-combining as a means to develop linguistic options. Outlines advantages of sentence-combining, presents examples of signaled and open exercises, recommends procedures for using them in the classroom.

THE PARAGRAPH

Braddock, Richard. "The Frequency and Placement of Topic Sentences in Expository Prose." *Research in the Teaching of English* 8 (1974): 287–302. • A survey of twenty-five essays from different kinds of publications reveals that fewer than half used topic sentences.

Christensen, Francis. *Notes Toward a New Rhetoric: Nine Essays for Teachers.* 2nd ed. New York: Harper, 1978. • A collection of essays on the structure of the sentence and the paragraph. [**21, 23–26, 29, 30, 32**]

――― . "A Generative Rhetoric of the Paragraph." *College Composition and Communication* 16 (Oct. 1965): 144–56. • Four principles that guide the rhetoric of the sentence are here applied to the paragraph. Each of nine characteristics of the paragraph is discussed. [**32**]

――― and Bonniejean Christensen. *A New Rhetoric.* New York: Harper, 1976. • Proceeds from a generative rhetoric of the sentence, emphasizing the cumulative sentence and beginning with description-narration, then moves to the paragraph and expository essays. [**21, 23–26, 29–30, 32**]

Meade, Richard A., and W. Geiger Ellis. "Paragraph Development in the Modern Age of Rhetoric." *English Journal* 59 (Feb. 1970): 219–26. • Examination of 300 randomly selected samples of actual writing reveals that textbooks recommend writing practices not followed by professional writers.

Pitkin, Willis L., Jr. "Discourse Blocs." *College Composition and Communication* 20 (May 1969): 138–48. • Connected discourse as a "hierarchy of discourse blocs."

SEMANTICS

Chase, Stuart. *The Tyranny of Words.* New York: Harcourt/Harvest, 1966. •
    Introduction to semantics. Includes examples of language abuse by econ-
    omists and politicians. [**19–21**]

Hayakawa, S. I. *Language in Thought and Action.* 4th ed. New York: Harcourt,
    1978. • Introduction to semantics. Includes chapters on report, infer-
    ence, and judgment; context; connotation; metaphor and simile; definition;
    classification. [**19, 23, 31, 32**]

A 5
B 6
C 7
D 8
E 9
F 0
G 1
H 2
I 3
J 4